THE CHRISTIAN SOLDIER OR Heaven Taken by Storm

Thomas Watson

A practical handbook on Christian living,
showing the holy violence a Christian is
to put forth in the pursuit after glory.

"The Kingdom of Heaven suffers violence, and
the violent take it by force." Matthew 11:12

CONTENTS

Introduction

John the Baptist, hearing in prison of the fame of Christ, sends two of his disciples to Him with this question, Are You He who should come, or do we look for another? verse 3. Not that John Baptist knew not that Jesus Christ was the true Messiah, for he was confirmed in this both by the Spirit of God and by a sign from heaven (John 1:33). But John the Baptist hereby endeavored to correct the ignorance of his own disciples who had a greater respect for him, than for Christ.

In the fourth verse Christ answers their question, "Go back and report to John what you hear and see: the blind receive sight, the lame walk, those who have leprosy are cured, the deaf hear, the dead are raised, and the good news is preached to the poor." Jesus Christ demonstrates Himself to be the true Messiah by His miracles which were real and visible proofs of His divinity. John's disciples being departed, Christ falls into a high praise and commendation of John the Baptist, Verse 7. "What did you go out into the desert to see? A reed swayed by the wind?" As if Christ had said, John the Baptist was no inconstant man, fluctuating in his mind and being shaken as a reed from one opinion to another; he was no Reuben, unstable as water—but was fixed and resolute in piety, and a prison could make no alteration in him.

Verse 8. "If not, what did you go out to see? A man dressed in fine clothes?" John did not indulge his senses; he wore not silks—but camel's hair; nor did he desire to live at court—but in a wilderness, Matt. iii. 3,4.

Again, Christ commends John as being His forerunner who prepared the way before him; verse 10. He was the morning star which preceded the Sun of Righteousness. And that Christ might sufficiently honor this holy man, He does not only parallel him with—but prefers him before, the chief of the prophets. Verse 9. "Then what did you go out to see? A prophet? Yes, I tell you, and more than a prophet. I tell you the truth: Among those born of women there has not risen anyone greater than John the Baptist." He was eminent both for dignity of office, and perspicuity of doctrine; and so our text is ushered in: "From the days of John the Baptist until now the kingdom of heaven suffers violence, and the violent take it by force." In these words there is,

1. The preface, or introduction: "from the days of John the Baptist until now." John the Baptist was a zealous preacher, a Boanerges, or son of Thunder; and after his preaching, people began to be awakened out of their sins.

Hence learn, what kind of **ministry** is likely to do most good, namely, that which works upon the consciences of men. John the Baptist lifted up his voice like a trumpet, he preached the doctrine of repentance with power, "Repent! for the kingdom of heaven is at hand!" Matt. 3:2. He came hewing and cutting down men's sins, and afterwards preached Christ to them. First, he poured in the *vinegar of the law*, then the *wine of the gospel*. This was that preaching which made men studiously seek after heaven. John did not so much preach to *please*—as to *profit*; he chose rather to reveal men's sins—than to show his own eloquence. The best mirror is not that which is most ornate—but that which shows the truest face. That preaching is to be preferred which makes the truest discovery of men's sins, and shows them their hearts. John the Baptist was a burning and shining light; he did burn in his doctrine and shine in his life; and therefore men pressed into heaven.

Peter, who was filled with a spirit of zeal, humbled his hearers for their sins, and opened to them a fountain in Christ's blood, they were pricked in their heart, Acts 2:37. It is the greatest mercy, to have a soul-searching ministry. If one had a desperate wound, he would desire to have it probed to the bottom. Who would not be content to have their souls searched, so they may have them saved?

2. The matter in the text: "The kingdom of heaven suffers violence, and the violent take it by force."

What is meant by *"the kingdom of heaven?"* Some interpret it as the doctrine of the gospel which reveals Christ and heaven. But I rather, by the kingdom of heaven, understand heavenly glory.

This kingdom *"suffers violence."* This is a metaphor from a town or castle which holds out in war, and is not taken—but by storm. So the kingdom of heaven will not be taken without violence: "The violent take it by force."

The *earth* is inherited by the *meek* Matt. 5:5. *Heaven* is inherited by the violent. Our life is military. Christ is our Captain, the gospel is the banner, the graces are our spiritual artillery, and heaven is only taken in a forcible way. These words fall into two parts.

1. The combat—suffers violence.

2. The conquest—the violent take it by force.

Doctrine: The right way to take heaven is by storm.
None get into heaven but violent ones.

This violence has a double aspect.

It concerns men as **MAGISTRATES**; they must be violent,

1. In punishing the guilty. When Aaron's Urim and Thummim will do no good, then must Moses come with his *rod*. The wicked are the bad blood and cancers of the commonwealth which, by the care of magistracy, are to be purged out. God has placed governors "for the terror of evildoers," 1 Peter ii. 14. They must not be like the sword-fish, which has a sword in his head but is without a heart. They must not have a sword in their hand—but no heart to draw it out for the cutting down of impiety. Lenience in a magistrate supports vice, and by not punishing offenders he adopts other men's faults and makes them his own. Magistracy without zeal is like the body without spirit. Too much leniency emboldens sin and does but shave the head, which deserves to be cut off!

2. In defending the innocent. The magistrate is the asylum or altar of refuge for the oppressed to fly to. Charles, Duke of Calabri, was so in love with doing justice that he caused a bell to be hung at his palace gate, and whoever would ring it, was sure presently to be admitted into the duke's presence, or have some officers sent out to hear his cause. Aristides was famous for his justice, of whom the historian says that he would never favor any man's cause because he was his friend, nor do injustice to any because he was his enemy. The magistrate's justice, is the oppressed man's shield.

This violence concerns men as **CHRISTIANS**. Though heaven is given us freely—yet we must contend for it, Eccles. ix. 10. "What your hand finds to do, do it with your might." Our *work* is great, our *time* short, our Master urgent. We have need therefore to summon together all the powers of our souls and strive as in a matter of life and death, that we may arrive at the kingdom above. We must not only put forth *diligence*—but *violence*. For the illustrating and clearing of this proposition, I will show.

1. What violence is <u>not</u> meant here: The violence in the text excludes,

*1. An **ignorant** violence;* to be violent for that which we do not understand, Acts xvii. 23. "As I passed by and beheld your devotions, I found an altar with this inscription—*to the unknown God.*" These Athenians were violent in their devotions—but it might be said to them, as Christ said to the woman of Samaria, John iv. 22. "You worship what you do not know." Thus the Catholics are violent in their religion. Witness their penance, fasting, lacerating themselves until the blood comes—but it is a zeal without knowledge; their mettle is better than their eye-sight. When Aaron was to burn incense upon the alter, he was first to light the lamps, Exod. xxv. 7. When zeal like incense burns, first the lamp of knowledge must be lighted.

*2. It excludes a **bloody** violence,* which is twofold:

First, when one goes to lay violent hands upon *himself*. The body is an earthly prison, where God has put the soul; we must not break prison—but stay until God lets us out by death. The sentinel is not to stir without permission from his captain; nor must we dare to stir hence without God's permission. Our bodies are the temples of the Holy Spirit, 1 Cor. Vi.19.; When we offer violence to them, we destroy God's temple: The lamp of life must burn so long as any natural moisture is left, like oil, to feed it.

Secondly, When one takes away the life of *another*. There's too much of this violence nowadays. No sin has a louder voice than blood, Gen iv. 10. The voice of your brother's blood cries unto Me from the ground. If there is a curse for him who *smites* his neighbor secretly, Deut. xxvii. 24, then he is doubly cursed who *kills* him. If a man had slain another unawares, he might take sanctuary and fly to the altar; but if he had done it willingly, the holiness of the place was not to protect him, Exod. xxi. 14, "But if a man schemes and kills another man deliberately, take him away from my altar and put him to death." Joab, being a man of blood, King Solomon sought to slay him even though he caught hold on the horns of the altar, 1 Kings viii. 29. In Bohemia, formerly, a murderer was to be beheaded and put in the same coffin with him whom he had killed. Thus we see what violence the text excludes.

2. What violence IS meant here—it is a HOLY violence. This is twofold.

1. We must be violent for the **TRUTH**. Here Pilate's question will be cited, "What is truth?" Truth is either the blessed Word of God which is called the Word of truth; or those doctrines which are deduced from the Word, and agree with it as the dial with the sun or the transcript with the original; as the doctrine of the Trinity, the doctrine of the creation, the doctrine of free grace, justification by the blood of Christ, regeneration, resurrection of the dead, and the life of glory. These truths we must be violent for, which is either by being advocates for them, or martyrs.

Truth is the most *glorious* thing; the least filing of this gold is precious—just so, with truth. What shall we be violent for, if not for truth? Truth is *ancient*; its grey hairs may make it venerable; it comes from him who is the ancient of days. Truth is *unerring*, it is the Star which leads to Christ. Truth is *pure*, Psalm 119. 140. It is compared to silver refined seven times, Psalm xii. 6. There is not the least spot on truth's face; it breathes nothing but sanctity. Truth is *triumphant*; it is like a great conqueror; when all his enemies lie dead, it keeps the field and sets up its trophies of victory. Truth may be opposed but never quite deposed. In the time of Diocletian things seemed desperate and truth ran low. Soon after was the golden time of Constantine, and then truth did again lift up its head. When the water in the Thames is lowest, a high tide is ready to come in. God is on truth's side and so long as there is no fear it will prevail:

The heavens being on fire shall be dissolved, 2 Peter iii. 12—but not that truth which came from Heaven, 1 Peter. i. 25.

Truth has noble effects. Truth is the seed of the new birth. God does not regenerate us by miracles or revelations—but by the Word of truth, James i. 18. As truth is the *breeder* of grace, so it is the *feeder* of it, 1 Tim. iv. 6. Truth *sanctifies*: John xvii. 17. Sanctify them through Your truth. Truth is the seal that leaves the print of its own holiness upon us; it is both a looking-glass to show us our blemishes, and a laver to wash them away. Truth makes us *free*, John xviii. 32. it bears off the fetters of sin and puts us into a state of Sonship, Romans viii.11, and Kingship, Rev. i. 6. Truth is *comforting*; this wine cheers. When David's harp could yield him no comfort, truth did, Psalm 119. 50. "This is my comfort in my affliction, for your Word has quickened me." Truth is an antidote against error. *Error is the adultery of the mind*; it stains the soul, as treason stains blood. Error damns as well as does vice. A man may as well die by poison—as by pistol; and what can stave off error but truth? The reason so many have been tricked into error is because they either did not know, or did not love, the truth. I can never say enough in the honor of truth. Truth is the ground of our faith; it gives us an exact model of piety; it shows us what we are to believe. Take away truth and our faith is fancy. Truth is the best flower in the church's crown; we have not a richer jewel to trust God with than our souls; nor He a richer jewel to trust us with than His truths. Truth is an ensign of honor; it distinguishes us from the false church, as chastity distinguishes a virtuous woman from an harlot. In short, truth is the bulwark a nation: 2 Chron. xi. 17. it is said, the Levites (who were the ensign bearers of truth) strengthened the kingdom. Truth may be compared to the capitol of Rome, which was a place of the greatest strength; or the Tower of David, on which "there hang a thousand shields," Cant. iv. 4. Our forts and navies do not so much strengthen us as truth. Truth is the best militia of a kingdom; if once we part with truth and espouse popery, the lock of hair is cut, where our strength lies. What then should we be violent for, if not for truth? We are bid to contend as in an agony "for the faith which was once delivered unto the saints," Jude verse 3. If truth once be gone, we may write this epitaph on England's tomb-stone, *"Your glory is departed!"*

2. This holy violence is also when we are violent for our own **SALVATION**, 2 Peter 1. 10. "Give diligence to make your calling and election sure." The Greek word signifies anxious carefulness, or a serious bearing of one's thoughts about the business of eternity, such a care as sets head and heart at work. In this channel of piety all a Christian's zeal should run.

3. The third thing is, what is implied in this holy violence? It implies three things:

1. Resolution of will.

2. Vigor of affection.

3. Strength of endeavor.

1. Resolution of the WILL. Psalm 119. 6. "I have sworn, and I will perform it, that I will keep your righteous judgments." Whatever is in the way to heaven, (though there be a lion in the way) I will encounter it like a resolute commander who charges through the whole body of the army. The Christian is resolved, come what will—that he will have heaven. Where there is this resolution, *danger* must be despised, *difficulties* trampled upon, *terrors* contemned. This is the first thing in holy violence: resolution of will. "I will have heaven whatever it costs me!" and this resolution must be in the strength of Christ.

Where there is but half a resolution—a will to be saved and a will to follow sin—it is impossible to be violent for Heaven. If a traveler be unresolved, sometimes he will ride this way, sometimes that; he is violent for neither.

2. Vigor of the AFFECTIONS. The will proceeds upon reason; the *judgment* being informed of the excellency of a state of glory; and the *will* being resolved upon a voyage to that holy land; now the *affections* follow and they are on fire in passionate longings after heaven. The affections are violent things, Psalm xlii. 2. "My soul thirsts for God, for the living God." The Rabbis note here, that David says *not*, "My soul hungers," but "thirsts," because naturally we are more impatient with thirst than hunger. See in what a rapid, violent motion David's affections were carried after God. Affections are like the wings of the bird which make the soul swift in its flight after glory; where the affections are stirred up, there is offering violence to heaven.

3. This violence implies strength of ENDEAVOR, when we strive for salvation as though a matter of life and death. It is easy to *talk* of Heaven—but not to *get* to Heaven! We must put forth all our strength, and call in the help of heaven to this work.

4. The fourth thing is, how many WAYS a Christian must offer violence: namely, four ways;

He must offer violence,

1. To Himself
2. To the World
3. To Satan
4. To Heaven

Ways a Christian must put forth holy violence

*"The Kingdom of Heaven suffers violence, and
the violent take it by force." Matthew 11:12*

1. The Christian must offer violence to HIMSELF.

This self-violence consists in two things:

1. Mortification of sin.

2. Provocation to duty.

1. Offering violence to one's self, in a spiritual sense, consists in mortification of sin: Self is the flesh; this we must offer violence to. Hierom, Chrysostom and Theophilact, do all expound taking Heaven by force, the mortifying of the flesh. The flesh is a bosom traitor; it is like the Trojan horse within the walls which does all the mischief. The flesh is a sly enemy; it kills by embracing. The embraces of the flesh are like the ivy embracing the oak; which sucks out the strength of it for its own leaves and berries. So the flesh by its soft embraces, sucks out of the heart all good, Gal. v. 17. The flesh lusts against the spirit. The pampering of the flesh, is the quenching of God's Spirit. The flesh chokes and stifles holy motions: the flesh sides with Satan and is true to its interest. There is a party within that will not pray, that will not believe. The flesh inclines us more to believe a temptation than a promise. There needs no wind to blow to sin when this tide within is so strong to carry us there. The flesh is so near to us, its counsels are more attractive. There is no chain of adamant which binds so tightly, as the chain of lust. Alexander, who was conqueror of the world, was led captive by vice. Now a man must offer violence to his fleshly desires if he will be saved, Col. iii. 5. "Mortify therefore your members which are upon the earth." The mortifying and killing sin at the root, is when we not only forbear the acts of sin—but hate the indwelling of sin. Put to death, therefore, whatever belongs to your earthly nature: sexual immorality, impurity, lust, evil desires and greed, which is idolatry. Colossians 3:5

Nay, where sin has received its deadly wound, and is in part abated—yet the work of mortification is not to be laid aside. The Apostle persuades the believing Romans to "mortify the deeds of the flesh, Romans viii.13. In the best of saints, there is something which needs mortifying; much pride, envy, and passion; therefore mortification is called crucifixion, Gal. v. 24. which is not done suddenly: every day some limb of the "body of death" must drop off. Nothing is harder than a rock, (says Cyril)—yet in the clefts thereof some *weed* or other will fasten its roots. None stronger than a believer—yet do what he can, sin will fasten its roots in him, and spring out sometimes with inordinate desires. There is always something which needs mortifying. Hence it was, that Paul did "beat down his body," by prayer, watching, and fasting, 1 Cor. ix. 27.

But, is it not said, Ephes. v. 29. "no man ever yet hated his own flesh?"

As flesh is taken *physically* for the bodily constitution, so it is to be cherished; but as flesh is taken *theologically* for the impure lustings of the flesh, so a man must hate his own flesh. The apostle says, "Fleshly lusts war against the soul," 1 Peter ii. 11. If the flesh does war against us—this is good reason, that we should war against the flesh.

How may one do to offer violence to himself in mortifying the flesh?

1. Withdraw the fuel that may make lust burn. Avoid all temptations. Take heed of that which nourishes sin. He who would suppress the gout or stone, avoids those meats which are noxious. Those who pray that they may not be led into temptation, must not lead themselves into temptation.

2. Fight against fleshly lusts with spiritual weapons—faith and prayer. The best way to combat with sin is—upon our knees. Run to the promise, Romans vi. 14. "Sin shall not have dominion over you:" or as the Greek word is, it shall not Lord it. Beg strength from Christ, Phil. ix. 13. Samson's strength lay in his *hair*; our strength lies in our *head*, Christ. This is one way of offering violence to one's self by mortification. This is a mystery to the major part of the world—who *gratify* the flesh rather than*mortify* it.

2. The second thing in offering violence to a man's self consists, is, in **provocation to duty**. Then we offer holy violence to ourselves when we excite and provoke ourselves to that which is good. This is called in Scripture, a 'stirring up ourselves to take hold of God," Isaiah lxiv. 7. Consider,

1. What absolute NEED there is to stir ourselves up to holy duties.

In respect to the sluggishness of our hearts, to that which is spiritual; blunt tools need sharpening; a dull creature needs spurs. Our hearts are dull and heavy in the things of God, therefore we have need to spur them on and provoke them to that which is good. The flesh hinders from duty: when we would pray, the flesh resists; when we should suffer, the flesh draws back. How hard it is sometimes to get the consent of our hearts to seek God! Jesus Christ went more willingly to the cross—than we do to the throne of grace. Had not we need then provoke ourselves to duty? If our hearts are so unstrung in piety, we had need prepare and put them in tune.

The exercises of God's worship are contrary to nature; therefore there must be a provoking of ourselves to them. The motion of the soul to sin is natural—but its motion towards holiness and Heaven is violent. The stone has an innate propensity downward; but to draw up a millstone into the air is done by violence, because it is against nature: so to lift up the heart to Heaven in duty, is done by violence and we must provoke ourselves to it.

2. What it is to provoke ourselves to duty.

1. It is to awaken ourselves, and shake off spiritual sloth. Holy David awakens his tongue and heart when he went about God's service, Psalm lvii. 9. "Awake up my glory, I myself will awaken early." He found a drowsiness and dullness in his soul, therefore did provoke himself to duty. "I myself will awake early." Christians, though they are raised from the death of sin—yet often they fall asleep.

Provoking ourselves to duty, implies an uniting, and rallying together all the powers of our soul, setting them on work in the exercises of piety. A man must say to his thoughts, "be fixed on God in this duty;" and to his affections, "serve the Lord without distraction." Matters of piety must be done with intenseness of spirit.

3. The third thing is to show the several DUTIES of Christianity, wherein we must provoke and offer violence to ourselves. I shall name seven.

1. We must provoke ourselves to READING of the Word. What an infinite mercy it is that God has blessed us with the Scriptures! The barbarous Indians have not the oracles of God made known to them; they have the golden mines—but not the Scriptures which are more to be desired "than much fine gold," Psalm xix. 10. Our Savior bids us "search the Scriptures", John v.39. We must not read these holy lines carelessly, as if they did not concern us, or run over them hastily, as Israel ate the Passover in haste; but peruse them with reverence and seriousness. The noble Bereans "searched the Scriptures daily," Acts xvii.11. The Scripture is the treasury of divine knowledge; it is the rule and touchstone of truth; out of this well we draw the water of life. To provoke to a diligent reading of the Word, labor to have a right notion of Scripture.

Read the Word as a book made by God Himself. It is given "by divine inspiration" 2 Tim. iii.16. It is the library of the Holy Spirit. The prophets and apostles were but God's amanuenses to write the law at his mouth. The Word is of divine original, and reveals the deep things of God to us. There is a sense of deity engraved in man's heart, and is to be read in the book of the creatures; but who this God is, and the Trinity of persons in the Godhead, is infinitely, above the light of reason; only God Himself could make this known. Just so, for the incarnation of Christ; God and man hypostatically united in one person; the mystery of imputed righteousness; the doctrine of faith: what angel in heaven, who but God himself, could reveal these things to us? How this may provoke to diligence and seriousness in reading the Word which is divinely inspired. Other books may be written by holy men—but this book is inspired by the Holy Spirit.

Read the Word as a perfect rule of faith; it contains all things essential to salvation. "I adore the fullness of Scripture," says Tertullian. The Word teaches us how to please God; how to order our lives in the world. It instructs us in all things that belong either to prudence or piety. How we should read the Word with care and reverence, when it contains a perfect model of piety and is "able to make us wise unto salvation" (2 Tim. 3:15)!

When you read the Word, look on it as a soul-enriching treasury. Search it as for hidden treasure! Proverbs 2:4. In this Word are scattered many divine sayings; gather them up as so many jewels. This blessed book will enrich you; it fills your head with divine knowledge, and your heart with divine grace; it stores you with promises: a man may be rich in bonds. In this field the pearl of price is hidden! What are all the world's riches compared to these? Islands of spices, coasts of pearl, rocks of diamonds? These are but the riches that reprobates may have—but the Word gives us those riches which angels have!

Read the Word as a book of evidences. How carefully does one read over his evidences! Would you know whether God is your God? search the records of Scripture, 1 John iii. 24. "Hereby we know that he abides in us." Would you know whether you are heirs of the promise? you must find it in these sacred writings. 2 Thes. ii. 13. "He has chosen us to salvation through sanctification." Those who are vessels of *grace*—shall be vessels of *glory!*

Look upon the Word as a spiritual armory, out of which you fetch all your weapons to fight against sin and Satan.

1. Here are weapons to fight against SIN. The Word of God is a holy sword, which cuts asunder the lusts of the heart! When pride begins to lift up itself, the sword of the Spirit destroys this sin! 1 Peter iv. 5 "God resists the proud." When passion vents itself, the Word of God, like Hercules's club, beats down this angry fury! Eccles. V. 9. "Anger rests in the bosom of fools." When lust boils, the Word of God cools that intemperate passion! Ephes. V. 5. "No unclean person has any inheritance in the Kingdom of Christ."

2. Here are weapons to fight against SATAN. The Word fences off temptation. When the devil tempted Christ, He wounded the old serpent three times with the sword of

the Spirit—"It is written!" Matt. iv. 7. Satan never sooner foils a Christian than when he is unarmed, and without Scripture weapons.

Look upon the Word as a spiritual looking-glass to dress yourselves by! It is a mirror for the blind, "The commands of the Lord are radiant, giving light to the eyes!" Psalm 19:8. In other mirrors you may see your *faces*; in this mirror you may see your*hearts!* Psalm 119. 104. "Through Your precepts I get understanding. This mirror of the Word clearly represents Christ; it sets him forth in his person, nature, offices, as most precious and eligible, Cant.vi. 16. "He is altogether lovely; he is a wonder of beauty, a paradise of delight. Christ who was veiled over in types, is clearly revealed in the mirror of the Scriptures.

Look upon the Word as a book of spiritual remedies and antidotes. Basil compares the Word to an apothecary's shop, which has all kinds of medicines and antidotes. If you find yourselves dead in duty, here is a receipt, Psalm 119. 50. "Your Word has quickened me." If you find your hearts hard, the Word does liquify and melt them; therefore it is compared to fire for its mollifying power, Jer. xxiii. 29. If you are poisoned with sin, here is an herb to expel it.

Look upon the Word as a sovereign elixir to comfort you in distress. It comforts you against all your sins, temptations, and afflictions. What are the promises—but divine cordials to revive fainting souls. A gracious heart goes feeding on a promise as Samson on the honeycomb, Judges xiv. 9. The Word comforts against sickness and death, 1 Cor xv. 55. "O death, where is your sting?" A Christian dies embracing the promise, as Simeon did Christ, Heb. xi. 13.

Read the Word as the last Will and Testament of Christ. Here are many legacies given to those who love him; pardon of sin, adoption, consolation. This will is in force, being sealed in Christ's blood. With what seriousness does a child read over the will and testament of his father, that he may see what is left him.

Read the Word as a book by which you must be judged: John xii. 48. "The Word that I have spoken shall judge him at the last day." Those who live according to the rules of this book, shall be acquitted; those who live contrary to them, shall be condemned. There are two books God will go by, the book of Conscience, and the book of Scripture: the one shall be the witness, and the other the judge. How should every Christian then provoke himself to read this book of God with care and devotion! This is that book which God will judge by at the last. Those who fly from the Word as a guide, shall be forced to submit to it as a judge.

2. The second duty of piety wherein we must provoke ourselves, is, in HEARING of the Word. We may bring our *bodies* to the preaching of the Word with ease—but not our *hearts,* without offering violence to ourselves. When we come to the Word preached, we come to a business of the highest importance, therefore should stir up ourselves and hear with the greatest devotion. Luke xix. 48. "All the people were very attentive to hear him." In the Greek it is "they hung upon his lip."—When the Word is dispensed, we are to lift up the everlasting doors of our hearts, that the King of glory may enter in!

1. How far are they from offering violence to themselves in hearing, who scarcely mind what is said, as if they were not at all concerned in the business. They come to church more for *custom,* than *conscience.* "My people come to you, as they usually do, and sit before you to listen to your words, but they do not put them into practice. With their mouths they express devotion, but their hearts are greedy for unjust gain. Indeed, to them you are nothing more than one who sings love songs with a beautiful voice and plays an instrument well, for they hear your words but do not put them into practice." Ezekiel 33:31-32. If we could tell them of a rich purchase, or of some place of worldly advancement, they would diligently attend; but when the Word of life is preached, they disregard it.

2. How far are they from offering violence to themselves in hearing, who come to the Word in a dull, drowsy manner—as if they came to church for the purpose of drowsing. The Word is to feed us; it is strange to sleep at the dinner table. The Word judges men; it is strange for a prisoner to fall asleep at the time of his sentencing. To such sleepy hearers God may say, "sleep on!" He may allow them to be so stupefied, that no ordinance shall them: Matt. iii. 25. "While men slept, his enemy came and sowed tares." The Devil is never asleep—but sows the *tares of sin* in a drowsy hearer.

That we may, when we come to the Word, offer violence to ourselves, and stir up ourselves to hear with devotion, consider,

1. That it is God himself, who speaks to us! If a *judge* gives a verdict upon the bench—all listen. If a *king* speaks—all pay attention. When we come to the Word, we should think thus with ourselves—we are to hear *God* in this preacher! Therefore Christ is said—to speak to us from Heaven, Heb. xii. 25. Christ speaks in his ministers, as a king speaks in the person of his ambassador. When Samuel knew it was the Lord who spoke to him, he lent an ear, 2. Sam. iii. 5. "Speak Lord, your servant hears!" Those who slight God speaking in His Word—shall hear him speaking to them in his wrath, Psalm ii. 5. "Then shall he speak unto them in his wrath!" "Depart from me, you who are cursed, into the eternal fire prepared for the devil and his angels!" Matthew 25:41.

2. Let us consider the weightiness of the matters delivered to us. As Moses said to Israel, Deut. xxx. 19. "I call Heaven and Earth to record this day, that I have set before you life and death." We preach to men of Christ and of eternal recompenses; here are the *weighty matters* of the law; and does not all this call for serious attention? There is a great deal of difference between a common news article read to us, and a letter of personal business, wherein our whole land and estate is concerned. In the Word preached our eternal salvation is concerned; here we are instructed to the kingdom of God, and if ever we will be serious, it should be now! Deut. xxxvii. 47. "It is not a vain thing for you, because it is your life."

3. If the Word is not regarded—it will not be remembered. Many complain they cannot remember; here is the reason, God punishes their *carelessness in hearing*—with *forgetfulness*. He allows Satan to take away the Word from them, Matt. xiii. 4. "The fowls of the air came and devoured the seed." The Devil always comes to church—but it is not with any good intent; he takes away the Word from men. How many have been robbed of the sermon and their souls both at once!

4. It may be the last time that God will ever speak to us in His Word. It may be the last sermon that ever we shall hear; and we may go from the place of hearing—to the place of damning. Did people think thus when they come into the house of God, "perhaps this will be the last time that God will counsel us about our souls, perhaps this is the last time that ever we shall see our minister's face," with what devotion would they come! how would their affections be all on fire in hearing? We give great attention to the last speeches of friends. A parent's dying words are received as oracles. Oh, let all this provoke us to diligence in hearing; let us think this may be the last time that Aaron's bell shall sound in our ears, and before another day—we shall be in another world!

3. The third duty wherein we are to offer violence to ourselves, is in PRAYER. Prayer is a duty which keeps the trade of piety flowing. When we either join in prayer with others, or pray alone, we must use holy violence. It is not *eloquence* in prayer—but *violence* carries it. Theodorus, speaking of Luther, "once (says he) I overheard Luther in prayer: with what life and spirit did he pray! It was with so much *reverence*, as if he were speaking to God—yet with so much *confidence*, as if he had been speaking to his friend." There must be a stirring up of the heart, 1. To prayer. 2. In prayer.

1. There must be a stirring up of the heart TO prayer, Job xi. 13. "If you prepare your heart, and stretch out your hands toward him." This preparing of our heart by holy thoughts and ejaculations. The musician first tunes his instrument, before he plays.

2. There must be a stirring up of the heart IN prayer. Prayer is a lifting up of the mind and soul to God, which cannot be done aright without offering violence to oneself. The names given to prayer imply violence. It is called *wrestling*, Gen. xxxii. 24. and a pouring out of the soul, 1 Sam. 1:15; both of which imply vehemency. The affection is required as well as invention. The apostle speaks of an effectual fervent prayer, which is a parallel phrase to offering violence.

1. Alas, how far from offering violence to themselves in prayer—are those who give God a **dead, heartless** prayer. God would not have the blind offered, Mal. 1:8; as good offer the *blind* is as offering the *dead*. Some are half asleep when they pray, and will a sleepy prayer ever awaken God? Such as mind not their own prayers, how do they think that God should mind them? Those prayers God likes best, which come seething hot from the heart.

2. Alas, how far are they from offering violence—are those who give God **distracted** prayer? while they are praying, they are thinking of their shop and trade. How can he shoot right whose eye is quite off the mark? Ezek. xxxiii. 31. "Their heart goes after their covetousness." Many are casting up their accounts in prayer, as Hieram once complained of himself. How can God be pleased with this? Will a king tolerate that, while his subject is delivering a petition, and speaking to him, he should be playing with a feather? When we send our hearts on an errand to Heaven, how often do they loiter and play by the way? This is a matter of blushing. That we may offer violence to ourselves and by fervency feather the wing of prayer, let these things be duly weighed.

1. The majesty of God with whom we have to do. He sees how it is with us in prayer, whether we are deeply affected with those things we pray for. "The king came in to see the guests," Matt. xxii.11. So when we go to pray, the King of glory comes in to see in what frame we are; he has a window which looks into our breasts, and if He sees a dead heart, he may turn a deaf ear. Nothing will sooner make God's anger wax hot, than a cold prayer.

2. Prayer without fervency and violence is no prayer; it is speaking, not praying. Lifeless prayer is no more prayer than the picture of a man is a man. To say a prayer, is not to pray; Ashanius taught his parrot the Lord's Prayer. It is the violence and wrestling of the affections that make it a prayer, else it is no prayer.

3. The zeal and violence of the affections in prayer best suits God's nature. He is a spirit, John iv. 24. and surely that prayer which is full of life and spirit is the savory food he loves, 1 Peter ii. 5. "Spiritual sacrifices acceptable to God." Spirituality and fervency in duty, is like the spirits of wine, which are the more refined part of the wine. Bodily exercise profits nothing. It is not the stretching of the lungs—but the vehemency of the desire, that makes music in God's ears.

4. Consider the need we have of those things which we ask in prayer. We come to ask the favor of God; and if we have not his love, all that we enjoy is cursed to us. We pray that our souls may be washed in Christ's blood, and if he washes us not, "we have no part in him." Such are these mercies that if God denies us, we are forever undone. Therefore what violence we need to put forth in prayer. When will a man be earnest, if not when he is begging for his life?

5. Let it provoke violence in prayer, to consider, that those things which we ask, God has a mind to grant. If a son asks nothing but what his father is willing to bestow, he may be the more earnest in his suit. We go to God for pardon of sin, and no work is more pleasing to him than to seal pardons. Mercy is his delight, Micah vii. 18. We pray to God for a holy heart, and this prayer is according to his will, 1 Thes. iv. 3. "This is the will of God, even your sanctification". We pray that God would give us a heart to love him. How pleasing must this request must be to God! This, if anything, may excite prayer, and carry it in a fiery chariot up to Heaven, when we know we pray for nothing but that which God is more willing to grant than we are to ask.

6. No mercy can be bestowed on us but in a way of prayer. Mercy is purchased by Christ's blood—but it is conveyed by prayer. All the promises are bonds made over to us—but prayer puts these bonds in suit. The Lord has told Israel with what rich mercy He would bespangle them; he would bring them to their native country, and that with new hearts, Ezek. xxxvi. *Yet this tree of the promise would not drop its fruit, until shaken with the hand of prayer*, verse 67. For "all this I will yet be inquired." The breast of God's mercy is full—but prayer must draw the breast. Surely, if all other ways are blocked up, there's no good to be done without prayer; how then should we ply this oar, and by a holy violence stir up ourselves to take hold of God.

7. It is only violence and intenseness of spirit in prayer that has the promise of mercy affixed to it. Matt vii. 7. "Knock, and it shall be opened." Knocking is a violent motion. The Aediles among the Romans had their doors always standing open, so that all who had petitions might have free access to them. God's heart is ever open to fervent prayer. Let us then be fired with zeal, and with Christ pray yet more earnestly. It is violence in prayer which makes Heaven-gates fly open, and fetches in whatever mercies we stand in need of.

8. Large returns God has given to violent prayer. The dove sent to Heaven has often brought an olive leaf in its mouth: Psalm xxxiv. 6. "This poor man *cried*, and the Lord heard him." Crying prayer prevails. Daniel in the den prayed and prevailed. Prayer shut the lion's mouth and opened the lion's den. Fervent prayer (says one) has a kind of omnipotency in it. Sozomen said of Apollonius, that he never asked anything of God in all his life, which he did not obtain. Sleidan reports of Luther, that perceiving the interest of piety to be low, he betook himself to prayer; at length rising off his knees, he came out of his closet triumphantly, saying to his friends, "We have overcome; we have overcome!" At which time it was observed that there came out a proclamation from Charles the Fifth, that none should be further molested for the profession of the gospel. How may this encourage us and make us hoist up the sails of prayer when others of the saints have had such good returns from the holy land.

That we may put forth this holy violence in prayer, it is requisite there be a renewed principle of grace. If the person is graceless, no wonder the prayer is heartless. The body while it is dead has no heat in it: while a man is dead in sin, he can have no heat in duty.

9. That we may be the more violent in prayer, it is good to pray with a sense of our needs. A beggar that is pinched with poverty, will be earnest in craving alms. Christian, review your needs; you need a humble, spiritual frame of heart; you need the light of God's countenance; the sense of need will quicken prayer. That man can never pray fervently who does not pray feelingly. How earnest was Samson for water when he was ready to die, Judges xv. 18. "I die for thirst!"

10. If we would be violent in prayer, let us beg for a violent wind. The Spirit of God is resembled to a mighty rushing wind, Acts ii. 2. Then we are violent, when this blessed wind fills our sails, Jude, verse 20, "Praying in the Holy Spirit." If any fire be in our sacrifice, it comes down from heaven.

The fourth duty wherein we must offer violence to ourselves is MEDITATION. This is a duty wherein the very heart and life-blood of piety lies. Meditation may be thus described: it is a holy exercise of the mind; whereby we bring the truths of God to remembrance, and do seriously ponder upon them and apply them to ourselves. In meditation there are two things:

1. A Christian's retiring of himself, a locking himself up from the world. Meditation is a work which cannot be done in a crowd.

2. It is a serious thinking upon God. It is not a few transient thoughts that are quickly gone—but a fixing and staying of the mind upon heavenly objects: this cannot be done without exciting all the powers of our souls, and offering violence to ourselves.

We are the more to provoke ourselves to this duty, because:

1. Meditation is so cross to flesh and blood. Naturally we shun holy meditation. To meditate on worldly, secular things, even if it were all day, we can do without any difficulty; but to have our thoughts fixed on God, how hard do we find it? How do our

hearts quarrel with this duty? What pleas and excuses we have to put it off? The natural averseness from this duty shows that we are to offer violence to ourselves in it.

2. Satan does what he can to hinder this duty. He is an enemy of meditation. The devil does not care not how much we read—so long as we do not meditate on what we read. Reading begets knowledge—but meditation begets devotion. Meditation stabilizes the heart and makes it serious, while Satan labors to keep the heart from being serious. What need therefore is there of offering violence to ourselves in this duty? But methinks I hear some say, when they sit alone they do not know what to meditate about. I shall therefore furnish them with matter for meditation.

1. Meditate seriously upon the CORRUPTION of your nature. We have lost that pure holy frame of soul that we once had. There is a sea of sin in us. Our nature is the source and seminary of all evil. It is like Peter's sheet, wherein were "wild beasts and creeping things," Acts x. 12. This sin cleaves to us as a leprosy. This original pollution makes us guilty before the Lord; and even though we would never commit actual sin, it merits hell. The meditation of this would be a means to pull down our pride. Nay, even those who have grace have cause to walk humbly because they have more corruption in them than grace: their dark side is broader than their light.

2. Meditate seriously upon the death and passion of CHRIST. His soul was overcast with a cloud of sorrow when he was conflicting with his Father's wrath; and all this we ourselves, should have suffered, Isaiah liii. 5. "He was wounded for our transgressions." As David said, "Lo, I have sinned—but these sheep, what have they done?" 2 Sam. xxiv. 17. So we have sinned—but this Lamb of God—what had he done?

The serious meditation of this would produce repentance. How could we look upon him "whom we have pierced," and not mourn over him? When we consider how dearly our sins cost Christ; how should we shed the blood of our sins which shed Christ's blood?

The meditation of Christ's death would fire our hearts with love to Christ. What friend shall we love, if not him who died for us? His love to us made him to be cruel unto himself. As Rebecca said to Jacob, Gen. xxvii. 13. "Upon me, be your curse." So said Christ, "upon me, be your curse," that poor sinners may inherit the blessing.

3. Meditate on your EVIDENCES for heaven. What have you to show for Heaven, if you should die this night?

1. Was your heart ever thoroughly convinced of sin? Did you ever see yourself lost without Christ? Conviction is the first step to conversion, John vii. 16.

2. Has God ever made you willing to take Christ upon his own terms? Zech vi. 13. "He shall be a priest upon his throne." Are you as willing that Christ should be upon the throne of your heart to rule you—as well as a priest at the altar to intercede for you? Are you willing to renounce those sins to which the bias of your heart does naturally incline? Can you set those sins, as Uriah, in the forefront of the battle to be slain? Are you willing to take Christ for better and for worse? to take him with his cross, and to avouch Christ in the worst of times?

3. Do you have the indwelling presence of the Spirit? If you have, what has God's Spirit done in you? Has he made you of another spirit? meek, merciful, humble? Is he a transforming Spirit? Has he left the impress of its holiness upon you? These are good evidences for Heaven. By these, as by a spiritual touchstone, you may know whether you have grace or not. Beware of false evidences. None are further from having the true pearl, than those who content themselves with the counterfeit.

4. Meditate upon the uncertainty of all earthly comforts. Creature-delights have their flux and reflux. How oft does the sun of worldly pomp and grandeur goes down at noon. Xerxes was forced to fly away in a small vessel, who but a little before lacked sea-room for his navy. We say everything is mutable; but who meditates upon it? The world is resembled to "a sea of glass mingled with fire" Rev. xv. 2. Glass is slippery; it has no sure footing; and glass mingled with fire is subject to consume. All creatures are fluid and uncertain, and cannot be made to fix. What is become of the glory of Athens, the pomp of Troy? 1 John ii.17. "The world passes away." It slides away as a ship in full sail. How quickly does the scene alter? and a low ebb follow a high tide? There's no trusting to anything. Health may turn to sickness; friends may die; riches may take wings. We are ever upon the tropics. The serious meditation of this, would, 1. Keep us from being so deceived by the world. We are ready to set up our rest here, Psalm xliv. 11. "Their inward thought is, that their houses shall continue forever!" We are apt to think that our mountain stands strong. We dream of an earthly eternity. Alas, if we would meditate on how casual and uncertain these things are, we should not be so often deluded. Have not we had great disappointments; and where we have thought to suck honey, there have we not drunk wormwood.

2. The meditation of the uncertainty of all things under the sun, would much moderate our affections to them. Why should we so eagerly pursue an uncertainty? Many take care to get a great estate; it is uncertain whether they shall keep it. The fire may break in where the thief cannot: or if they do keep it, it is a question whether they shall have the comfort of it. They lay up for a child; that child may die; or if he live, he may prove a burden. This seriously meditated on, would cure the swelling of covetousness; and make us sit loose to that which hangs so loose and is ready to drop from us.

3. The meditation of this uncertainty would make us look after a certainty: that is, the getting of grace. This holy "anointing abides," 1 John ii. 27. Grace is a flower of eternity. Death does not destroy grace but transplant it and makes it grow in better soil. He who has true holiness can no more lose it than the angels can, who are fixed stars in glory.

5. Meditate on God's severity against SIN. Every arrow in God's quiver is shot against sin. Sin burned Sodom, and drowned the old world. Sin kindles hell. If when a spark of God's wrath flies into a mans conscience, it is so terrible, what is it when God 'stirs up all his wrath"? Psalm lxxviii. 38. The meditation of this would frighten us out of our sins. There cannot be so much sweetness in sin—as there is sting. How dreadful is God's anger! Psalm xc. 11. "Who knows the power of his wrath?" All fire, compared with the fire of God's wrath, is but painted and imaginary fire. O that every time we meddle with sin, we would think to ourselves we choose the bramble, and fire will come out of this bramble to devour us.

6. Meditate on ETERNAL LIFE. 1 John ii. 25. "This is his promise, even eternal life." Life is sweet, and this word *eternal* makes it sweeter. This lies in the immediate vision and fruition of God.

1. This is a **spiritual** life. It is opposite to that animal life which we live now. Here we hunger and thirst; but there we "shall hunger no more" Rev. vii. 16). There is the marriage supper of the Lamb, which will not only satisfy hunger—but prevent it. That blessed life to come does not consist in sensual delights, food, and drink, and music; nor in the comfort of relations; but the soul will be wholly swallowed up in God, and acquiesce in him with infinite delight. As when the sun appears, the stars vanish, so when God shall appear in his glory and fill the soul, then all earthly sensitive delights shall vanish.

2. It is a **glorious** life. The bodies of the saints shall be enameled with glory: they shall be made like Christ's glorious body, Phil. iii. 21. And if the cabinet be of such curious needle-work, how rich shall the jewel be that is put into it! how bespangled with glory shall the soul be! Every saint shall wear his white robe, and have his throne to sit upon. Then God will put some of his own glory upon the saints. Glory shall not only be revealed to them—but in them, Romans viii.18. And this life of glory shall be crowned with eternity; what angel can express it! O let us often meditate on this.

1. Meditation on eternal life would make us labor for a spiritual life. The child must be born before it is crowned. We must be born of the Spirit; before we are crowned with glory.

2. The meditation on eternal life would comfort us in regard to the shortness of natural life. Our life we live now, flies away as a shadow: it is called a flower, Psalm ciii. 15. a vapor, James iv. 14. Job sets forth fragile life very elegantly in three of the elements, land, water, and air, Job ix. 25,26. Go to the land, and there man's life is like a swift *runner*. Go to the water, there man's life is like a *ship* under sail. Look to the air, and there man's life is like a flying *eagle*. We are hastening to the grave. When our years do increase, our life does decrease. Death creeps upon us by degrees. When our *sight* grows dim, there death creeps in at the eye. When our *hearing* is bad, death creeps in at the ear. When our *legs* tremble under us, death is pulling down the main pillars of the house: but eternal life comforts us against the shortness of natural life. That life to come is subject to no infirmities; it knows no end. We shall be as the angels of God, capable of no mutation or change. Thus you have seen six noble subjects for your thoughts to expatiate upon.

But where is the meditating Christian? I lament the lack of holy meditation. Most people live in a hurry; they are so distracted with the cares of the world, that they can find no time to meditate or scarcely ask their souls how they do. We are not like the saints in former ages. David meditated in God's precepts, Psalm 119. 15. "Isaac walked in the evening to meditate," Gen. xxiv. 63. He did take a stroll with God. What devout meditations do we read in Austin and Anselm? But it is too much out of date among our modern professors.

Those beasts under the law which did not chew the cud, were unclean. Such as do not chew the cud by holy meditation are to be reckoned among the unclean. But I shall rather turn my lamentation into a persuasion, entreating Christians to offer violence to themselves in this necessary duty of meditation. Pythagoras sequestered himself from all society, and lived in a cave for a whole year, that he might meditate upon philosophy. How then should we retire and lock up ourselves at least once a day, that we may meditate upon glory.

1. Meditation makes the Word preached to profit; it works it upon the conscience. As the bee sucks the honey from the flower, so by meditation we suck out the sweetness of a truth. It is not the receiving of food into the mouth—but the digesting of it which makes it nutritious. So it is not the receiving of the most excellent truths in at the ear, which nourishes our souls—but the digesting of them by meditation. Wine poured in a sieve, runs out. Many truths are lost, because ministers pour their wine into sieves, either into leaking memories or feathery minds. Meditation is like a soaking rain, that goes to the root of the tree, and makes it bring forth fruit.

2. Holy meditation quickens the affections. "Oh, how I love your law! I meditate on it all day long." Psalm 119:97. The reason why our affections are so cold to heavenly things, is because we do not warm them at the fire of holy meditation. As the musing on worldly objects makes the fire of *lust* burn; the musing on injuries makes the fire of *revenge* burn; just so, meditating on the transcendent beauties of Christ, would make our love to Christ flame forth.

3. Meditation has a transforming power in it. The hearing of the Word may affect us—but the meditating upon it does transform us. Meditation stamps the impression of divine truths upon our hearts. By meditating on God's holiness, we grow holy. As Jacob's cattle, by looking on the rods, conceived like the rods: so while by meditation we look upon God's purity, we are changed into his likeness and are made partakers of his divine nature.

4. Meditation produces reformation. Psalm 119:59. "I have considered my ways and have turned my steps to your statutes." Did but people meditated on the damnableness of sin; they would realize that there is a rope at the end of it, which will hang them eternally in hell; they would break off a course of sinning, and become new creatures. Let all this persuade us to holy meditation. I dare be bold to say that if men would spend but one quarter of an hour every day in contemplating heavenly objects, it would leave a mighty impression upon them, and, through the blessing of God might prove the beginning of a happy conversion.

But how shall we be able to meditate?

Get a love for spiritual things. We usually meditate on those things which we love. The voluptuous man can muse on his pleasures: the covetous man on his bags of gold. Did we love heavenly things, we would meditate more on them. Many say they cannot meditate, because they lack memory; but is it not rather because they lack love? Did they love the things of God, they would make them their continual study and meditation.

5. The fifth duty wherein we are to offer violence to ourselves, is SELF-EXAMINATION. "Examine yourselves to see whether you are in the faith; test yourselves. Do you not realize that Christ Jesus is in you—unless, of course, you fail the test?" 2 Corinthians 13:5. This is a duty of great importance: it is a parleying with one's own heart, Psalm lxxxvii. 7. "I commune with my own heart." David did put interrogatories to himself. Self-examination is the setting up a court, in conscience and keeping a register there, that by strict scrutiny a man may know how things stand between God and his own soul. Self-examination is a spiritual inquisition; a bringing one's self to trial. A good Christian does as it were, begin the day of Judgment here in his own soul. Self-searching is a heart-anatomy. As a surgeon, when he makes a dissection in the body, discovers the inward parts, the heart, liver, and arteries—just so, a Christian anatomizes himself; he searches what is flesh and what is spirit; what is sin, and what is grace, Psalm lxxvii. 7. "My spirit made diligent search." As the woman in the Gospel did light a candle, and search for her lost coin, Luke xv. 8—so conscience "is the candle of the Lord," Proverbs xx. 27. A Christian by the light of this candle must search his soul to see if he can find any grace there.

The rule by which a Christian must try himself, is the Word of God. Sentimentality and public opinion are false rules to go by. We must judge of our spiritual condition by the rule of Scripture. This David calls a "lamp unto his feet," Psalm 119. 105. Let the Word be the umpire to decide the controversy, whether we have grace or not. We judge of colors by the sun. So we must judge of the state of souls by the light of Scripture.

Self-examination is a great and necessary duty; it requires self-excitation; it cannot possibly be done without offering violence to ourselves. 1. Because the duty of self-examination in itself is difficult: 1. It is a work of self-reflection; it lies most with the heart. It is hard to look inward. External acts of religion are easy; to lift up the eye to Heaven, to bow the knee, to read a prayer—this requires no more labor than for a Catholic to count over his beads; but to examine a man's self, to turn in upon his own soul, to take the heart as a watch all in pieces, and see what is defective; this is not easy. Reflective acts are hardest. The eye can see everything but itself. It is easy to spy the faults of others—but hard to find out our own.

2. Examination of a man's self is difficult, because of self-love. As ignorance blinds, so self-love flatters. Every man is ready to think the best of himself. What Solomon says of love to our neighbor is most true of self-love; "it hides a multitude of sins," Proverbs x.12. When

a man looks upon himself in the looking-glass of self-love, his virtues appear greater than they are, and his sins less. Self-love makes one rather excuse what is amiss, than examine it.

2. As examination is in itself difficult, so it is a work which we are very hardly brought to. That which causes a backwardness to self-examination, is,

1. Consciousness of guilt. Sin clamors inwardly, and men are loathe to look into their hearts lest they should find that which should trouble them. It is little pleasure to read the hand writing on the wall of conscience. Many Christians are like tradesmen who are sinking in their estates; they are loathe to look over their books, or cast up their accounts, lest they should find their estates low: so they are loathe to look into their guilty heart, lest they should find something there which should affright them; as Moses was affrighted at the sight of the rod turned into a serpent.

2. Men are hardly brought to this duty because of foolish, presumptuous hopes: they fancy their estate to be good, and while they weigh themselves in the balance of presumption, they pass the test. Many take their salvation on trust. The foolish virgins thought they had oil in their lamps, the same as the wise, Matt. xxv. Some are not sure of their salvation—but secure. If one were to buy a piece of land, he would not take it upon trust—but examine the title. How confident are some of salvation—yet never examine their title to Heaven.

3. Men are not forward to examine themselves, because they rest in the good opinions of others: how vain this is! Alas, one may be gold and pearl in the eye of others—yet God may judge him reprobate silver! Others may think him a saint, and God may write him down in his black-book. Judas was looked upon by the rest of the Apostles as a true believer—yet he was a traitor. Bystanders can but see the outward behavior—but they cannot tell what evil is in the heart. Fair streams may run on the top of a river—but vermin may lay at the bottom.

4. Men are hardly brought to examine themselves, because they do not believe Scripture. The Scripture says, "The heart is deceitful above all things and beyond cure. Who can understand it?" Jeremiah 17:9. Solomon said there were four things too astonishing for him, that he could not know. Prov xxx. 19. He might have added a fifth. The way of a man's heart. The heart is the greatest impostor; it will be ready to put one off with seeming grace, instead of saving. The heart will persuade that a slight tear is repentance; a lazy desire is faith. Now because the generality of people do not believe that there is such fallacy in their hearts, therefore they are so slow to examine them. This natural backwardness in us to self-reflection, should cause us to offer the more violence to ourselves in making a thorough investigation and search of our hearts.

O that I might prevail with Christians to take pains with themselves in this great work of examination. Their salvation depends on it. It is the wat of a harlot—she is seldom at home, Proverbs vii. 11,12. "her feet never stay at home; now in the street, now in the squares, at every corner she lurks." It is a sign of an harlot-professor, to be always abroad, spying the faults of others; but is never at home with his own heart. Oh let us try our hearts, as we try gold, by the touch-stone. Let us examine our sins, and finding out this leaven, burn it. Let us examine our grace, whether it be of the right kind. One went into the field to gather herbs, and he gathered wild gourds—and then death was in the pot, 2Kings iv. 40. So many think they have grace, the right herb; but it proves a wild gourd, and brings death and damnation. That we may offer violence to ourselves in this great business of examination, let these few things be seriously weighed.

1. Without self-examination we can never know how it is with us. If we would die presently, we cannot tell to what coast we should sail; whether to hell or Heaven. It is

reported of Socrates, when he was going out of the world, he had this speech, I am now to die, and the gods alone know whether I shall be happy or miserable. That man who is ignorant of the state of his soul, must needs have the trembling at the heart, as Cain had a shaking in his body. By a serious scrutiny of our hearts, we come to know to what prince we belong, whether to the prince of peace, or the prince of darkness.

2. If we will not examine ourselves, God will examine us. He will examine us, as the chief captain did Paul, by scourging, Acts xxii. 24. He will ask the same question as Christ, "whose is this image and superscription?" And if we cannot show him His own image, he will reject us.

3. There is secret corruption within, which will never be found out but by searching. "There is in the heart" (as Austin said) "hidden pollution." When Pharaoh's steward accused Joseph's brethren of having the cup, they dared have sworn they did not have the cup in their sack. Little does a man know what secret atheism, pride, and lust is in his heart until he searches.

4. The great advantage will accrue to us: the benefit is great whichever way things turn. If upon examination we find that we have not saving grace—then the mistake is discovered, and the danger can be prevented. If we find that we have saving grace— we may take the comfort of it. How glad was he who had "found the pearl of great price?" He who upon search finds that he has but the least degree of grace, is like one who has found his box of evidences; he is heir to all the promises, and in a state of salvation!

And that we may go on the more successively in this work, let us desire God to help us to find out our hearts, Job xxxiv. 32. "That which I see not teach you me."—Lord, take off the veil; show me my heart; let me not perish through mistake, or go to hell with hope of Heaven. "Search me, O God, and know my heart; test me and know my anxious thoughts. See if there is any offensive way in me, and lead me in the way everlasting." Psalm 139:23-24.

6. The sixth duty wherein we must offer violence to ourselves, is HOLY CONVERSE. Indeed we are backward enough to it, therefore had need to provoke ourselves, Mal. iii. 17. "They that feared the Lord spoke often one to another." A gracious person has not only piety only in his heart—but also in his tongue, Psalm xxxvii. 30. "The law of God is in his heart, and his tongue talks of judgment:" he drops holy words as pearls. It is the fault of Christians, that they do not in company provoke themselves to good discourse: it is a sinful modesty; there is much visiting— but they do not give one another's souls a visit. In worldly things their tongue is as the pen of a ready writer—but in matters of piety, it is as if their tongue did cleave to the roof of their mouth. As we must answer to God for idle words: so also for sinful silence.

Oh let us offer violence to ourselves on this, in initiating good discourse! What should our words dilate and expiate upon but Heaven? The world is a great Inn; we are guests in this Inn. Travelers, when they are met in their Inn, do not spend all their time in speaking about their Inn; they are to lodge there but a few hours, and are gone; but they are speaking of their home, and the country wither they are traveling. So when we meet together, we should not be talking only about the world; we are to leave this presently; but we should talk of our heavenly country, Heb. xi. 16.

That we may provoke ourselves to good discourse (for it will not be done without some kind of violence) let these considerations be duly weighed.

"The good man brings good things out of the good stored up in his heart, and the evil man brings evil things out of the evil stored up in his heart. For out of the overflow of his heart his mouth speaks." Luke 6:45. The discourse demonstrates what the heart is. As the looking-glass shows what the face is—whether it be fair or foul; just so, our words show what our heart is. Vain discourse reveals a light, feathery heart. Gracious discourse reveals a gracious heart. The water of the conduit shows what the spring is.

Holy discourse is very edifying. The apostle bids us "edify one another," Ephes. iv. 20. And how more than in this way? Godly discourse enlightens the mind when it is ignorant; settles it when it is wavering. A good life adorns piety; godly discourse propagates it.

Gracious discourse makes us resemble Christ. His words were perfumed with holiness: "grace was poured into his lips," Psalm 45:2. He spoke to the admiration of all: his hands worked miracles and his tongue spoke oracles, Luke iv. 22. "All bare him witness, and wondered at the gracious words which proceeded out of his mouth." Christ never came into any company—but he set good discourse on foot. Levi made him a feast, Luke v. 29. and Christ feasted him with holy discourse. When he came to Jacob's well, he presently speaks of the "water of life," Jude 4. The more holy our discourse is, the more we are like Christ. Should not the members be like the head?

God takes special notice of every good word we speak when we meet. "Then those who feared the Lord talked with each other, and the Lord listened and heard. A scroll of remembrance was written in his presence concerning those who feared the Lord and honored his name." Malachi 3:16. Tamerlain, that Scythian captain, had always a book by him of the names and good deserts of his servants which he bountifully rewarded. As God has a bottle for the tears of his people—so he has a book in which he writes down all their good speeches, and will make honorable mention of them at the last day. "Let your conversation be always full of grace, seasoned with salt, so that you may know how to answer everyone." Colossians 4:6

Holy discourse will be a means to bring Christ into our company. The two disciples were communing of the death and sufferings of Christ; and while they were speaking, Jesus Christ came among them, Luke xxiv. 15. "While they communed together, Jesus himself drew near, and went with them." When men entertain bad discourse, Satan draws near, and makes one of the company; but when they have holy and gracious discourse, Jesus Christ draws near, and wherever he comes, he brings a blessing along with him. So much for the first directive—the offering of violence to **ourselves**.

2. The Christian must offer violence to SATAN. Satan opposes us both by open violence, and secret treachery. Satan opposes by open violence—so he is called the *Red Dragon*. Satan opposes by secret treachery—so he is called the *Old Serpent*. We read in Scripture of his *snares* and *darts*; he hurts more by his snares than by his darts.

1. His VIOLENCE. He labors to storm the castle of the heart; he stirs up passion, lust, and revenge. These are called "fiery darts," Ephes. vi.16 because they often set the soul on fire. Satan in regard to his fierceness, is called a **lion**, "Be self-controlled and alert. Your enemy the devil prowls around like a roaring lion looking for someone to devour!" 1 Peter 5:8. Not whom he may *bite*—but *devour*.

2. His TREACHERY. What he cannot do by force, he will endeavor to do by fraud. Satan has several subtle devices in tempting:

1. In suiting his temptations to the temper of the individual. Satan studies our constitutions, and lays suitable baits. He knew Achan's s covetous heart, and tempted him with a wedge of gold. He tempts the youthful man with lust.

2. Another of Satan's subtleties, is to draw men to evil, under a pretense of good. The pirate does mischief by hanging out false colors; so does Satan by hanging out the colors of religion. He puts some men upon sinful actions, and persuades them much good will come of it. He tells them in some cases that they may dispense with the rule of the Word, and stretch their conscience beyond that line, that they may be in a capacity of doing more service—as if God needed our sin to raise his glory!

3. Satan tempts to sin gradually. As the farmer digs about the root of a tree, and by degrees loosens it, and at last it falls. Satan steals into into the heart by degrees. He is at first more modest. He did not say to Eve at first, "Eat the apple!" No! but he goes more subtly to work; he puts forth a *question*. "Has God said? Surely Eve, you are mistaken; the bountiful God never intended to debar one of the best trees of the garden. Has God said? Surely, either God did not say it; or if he did, he never really intended it." Thus by degrees he wrought her to distrust God, and then she took of the fruit and ate. Oh, take heed of Satan's first motions to sin, which seem more modest. He is first a *fox*, and then a *lion*.

4. Satan tempts to evil in lawful things. It was lawful for Noah to eat the fruit of the grape; but he took too much, and so sinned. Excess turns that which is good—into evil. Eating and drinking may turn to intemperance. Industry in one's calling, when excessive, becomes covetousness. Satan draws men to an immoderate love of the creature, and then makes them sin in that which they love—as Agrippina poisoned her husband Claudius in that food which he loved most.

5. Satan puts men upon doing good out of evil ends. If he cannot hurt them by scandalous actions, he will by virtuous actions. Thus he tempts some to espouse religion out of ulterior motives; and to give to charity, for applause, that others may see their good works. This hypocrisy does leaven the duties of religion and makes them lose there reward.

6. The Devil persuades men to evil, by such as are good. This sets a gloss upon his temptations, and makes them less suspected. The devil has made use sometimes of the most eminent and holy men to promote his temptations. The devil tempted Christ by an apostle, Peter dissuades him from suffering. Abraham, a good man, bids his wife equivocate; Say, you are my sister.

These are Satan's subtleties in tempting. Now here we must offer violence to Satan,

1. By FAITH. "Resist him, standing firm in the faith." 1 Peter 5:9. Faith is a wise, intelligent grace: it can see a hook under the bait. 2. It is an heroic grace; it is said above all, to quench the fiery darts of Satan. Faith resists the devil. "Take up the shield of faith, with which you can extinguish all the flaming arrows of the evil one!" Ephesians 6:16

1. Faith keeps the castle of the heart, so that it does not yield. It is not being tempted which makes us guilty--but giving consent. Faith enters its protest against Satan.

2. Faith not only not yields—but beats back the temptation. Faith holds the promise in one hand, and Christ in the other: The promise encourages faith, and Christ strengthens it: so faith beats the enemy out of the field.

2. We must offer violence to Satan by PRAYER. We overcome him upon our knees. As Samson called to Heaven for help, so a Christian by prayer fetches in auxiliary forces from Heaven. In all temptations, go to God by prayer. "Lord, teach me to use every piece of the spiritual armor; how to hold the shield, how to wear the helmet, how to use the sword of the Spirit. Lord, strengthen me in the battle; let me rather die a conqueror than be taken prisoner, and led by Satan in triumph!" Thus we must offer violence to Satan. There is "a lion in the way," but we must resolve upon fighting.

And let this encourage us to offer violence to Satan. Our enemy is beaten in part already. Christ, who is "the captain of our salvation," has given Satan his death-wound upon the cross, Col. ii. 15. The serpent is soonest killed in his head. Christ has bruised the head of the old Serpent! He is a chained enemy, and a conquered enemy; therefore do not fear him. "Resist the devil, and he will flee from you!" James 4:7. "The God of peace will soon crush Satan under your feet!" Romans 16:20.

3. The Christian must offer violence to the WORLD. The world shows its golden apple. It is a part of our Christian profession, to fight under Christ's banner against the world. Take heed of being drowned in the world's luscious delights! It must be a strong brain that can bear heady wine. He had need have a great deal of wisdom and grace who knows how to maintain a great estate. Riches often send up intoxicating fumes, which make men's heads giddy with pride. "Jeshurun waxed fat and kicked," Deut. xxxi. 15. It is hard to climb up the hill of God, with too many *golden weights*. Those who desire the *honors* of the world—receive the *temptations* of it. The world is a flattering enemy. It is given to some, as Michal to David, for a snare. The world shows its two breasts of **pleasure** and **profit**—and many fall asleep with the breast in their mouth! The world never kisses us—except with an intent to betray us. The world is a silken halter. The world is no friend to grace; it chokes our love to heavenly things—the *earth* puts out the *fire*.

Naturally we love the world, Job xxxi. 24. "If I have made gold my hope;" the Septuagint renders it, "If I have been married to my gold." Too many are wedded to their money; they live together as man and wife. O let us take heed of being entangled in this pleasing snare! Many who have escaped the rock of scandalous sins—yet have sunk in the world's golden quicksands! The sin is not in *using* the world—but in *loving* it. 1 John 2:15. "Do not love the world or anything in the world. If anyone loves the world, the love of the Father is not in him."

If we are Christians, we must offer violence to the world. Believers are called out of the world. "They are not of the world, even as I am not of it." John 17:16. They are **in** the world—but not **of** it. As we say of a dying man, he is not a man for this world. A true saint is crucified in his affections to the world, Gal. 6:14. He is dead to the honors and pleasures or it. What delight does a dead man take in pictures or music? Jesus Christ gave himself "to redeem us from this present evil world," Gal. 1:4. If we will be saved, we must offer violence to the world. Living fish swim against the stream. We must swim against the world, else we shall be carried down the stream, and fall into the dead sea of hell. That we may offer violence to the world, let us remember:

1. The world is **DECEITFUL**. Our Savior calls it, "The deceitfulness of riches," Matt. 13:22. The world promises happiness—but give less. It promises us Rachel—but gives us bleary-eyed Leah. The world *promises to satisfy* our desires—but only*increases* them. The world gives poisoned pills—but wraps them in sugar!

2. The world is **POLLUTING**. "Religion that God our Father accepts as pure and faultless is this: . . . to keep oneself from being **polluted** by the world." James 1:27 As if the apostle would intimate that the world is good for nothing but to pollute. It first pollutes men's consciences, and then their names. It is called filthy lucre, Titus 1:7. because it makes men so filthy. They will damn themselves to get the world. Ahab would have Naboth's vineyard, though he swam to it in blood.

3. The world is **PERISHING**. "The world and its desires pass away." 1 John 2:17. The world is like a flower which withers while we are smelling it!

4. Fourthly, the Christian must offer violence to HEAVEN. "The kingdom of Heaven suffers violence." Though Heaven is given us freely—yet we must take pains for it. Canaan was given Israel freely—but they had to fight with the Canaanites. It is not a lazy wish, or a sleepy prayer, which will bring us to Heaven; we must offer violence. Therefore in Scripture our earnestness for Heaven is shown by those allegories and metaphors which imply violence.

1. Sometimes by **striving**. Luke 13:23-24. "Someone asked him, "Lord, are only a few people going to be saved?" He said to them, "**Make every effort** to enter through the narrow door, because many, I tell you, will try to enter and will not be able to." (The Greek signifies, "Strive as in an agony.")

2. **Wrestling**, which is a violent exercise. Eph. 6:12. We are to wrestle with a body of sin, and with the powers of hell.

3. **Running** in a race, 1 Cor. 9:24. "So run that you may obtain." We have a long race from earth to Heaven—but a little time to run; it will soon be sunset. Therefore, so run. In a race there's not only a laying aside of all weights that hinder—but a putting forth of all the strength of the body; a straining every joint that men may press on with

all swiftness to lay hold on the prize. Thus Paul pressed towards the mark. Phil. iii:14. Alas, where is this holy violence to be found?

1. Many have made themselves *unfit* to run this blessed race; they are drunk with the pleasures of the world. A drunken man is unfit to run a race.

2. Others *neglect* to run this race all their life; and when sickness and death approach, now they will begin. A sick man is very unfit to *walk*, much less to *run* a race. I acknowledge that true repentance is never too late; but when a man can hardly move his hand, or lift up his eyes—that is a very unfit time to begin the race from earth to Heaven.

3. This earnestness for heaven is compared to **fighting**, which implies violence, 1 Tim. vi. 12. "Fight the good fight of faith." It is not enough to be laborers; we must be warriors. Indeed, in Heaven, our armor shall be hung up as a token of victory; but now it is a day of battle; and we must "fight the good fight of faith." As Hannibal forced a way for his army over the Alps and craggy rocks; so must we force our way to Heaven. We must not only pray—but pray fervently, James vi.16. This is offering violence to Heaven.

The reasons why there must be this offering violence to Heaven are:

1. God's indispensable command. He has enacted a law, that whoever eats of the fruit of paradise, shall eat it in the sweat of his brow. 2 Peter i. 10. "Give diligence to make your calling and election sure."

2. God's decree. The Lord has in his eternal decree joined the end and the means together: striving and entering, the race and the crown. And a man can no more think to come to Heaven without offering violence, than he can think to come to the end of his journey, who never sets a step in the way. Who expects an harvest without plowing and sowing? How can we expect the harvest of glory without labor? Though our salvation with respect to Christ is a purchase—yet with respect to us, it is a conquest.

3. We must offer violence to Heaven in regard to the difficulty of the work: Taking a kingdom. First, we must be pulled out of another kingdom, "The kingdom of darkness," Acts xxvi.18. To get out of the state of nature is hard, and when that is done, and we are cut off from the wild olive tree, and implanted into Christ, there is new work still to do; new sins to mortify; new temptations to resist, new graces to quicken. A Christian must not only get faith—but go "from faith to faith," Romans i. 17. This will not be done without violence.

4. We must offer violence to Heaven in regard to the violent assaults made against us.

1. Our own **hearts** oppose us. It is is a strange paradox: man, who does naturally desire happiness—yet opposes it; he desires to be saved—yet hates that holy violence which would save him.

2. All the powers of **hell** oppose us. Satan stands at our right hand, as he did at Joshua's, Zech. iii. Shall we not be as earnest to save our souls, as the dragon is to devour them? Without violent affections we shall never resist violent temptations.

5. We must be violent, because it is a matter of the highest importance. A man does not beat his head about trifles—but about matters wherein his life and estate are concerned. Violence is to be offered, if we consider:

1. What we shall **save**: the precious *soul*. What pains do we take for the feeding and enriching of the body, the brutish part? O then what violence should we use for the saving of the soul? The body is but a ring of clay; the soul is the diamond. The soul is the mirror wherein the image of God is seen. There are in the soul some shadows and faint representations of a deity. If Christ thought the soul was worth the shedding of His blood, well may we think it worth spending our sweat.

2. Consider what we shall **gain**: a *kingdom*. What pains are used for earthly crowns and empires; men will wade to the crown through blood. Heaven is a kingdom which should make us strive for it—even to blood. The hopes of a kingdom (says Basil) should carry a Christian cheerfully through all labors and sufferings.

There must be an offering of violence in regard to that aptness and proneness in the best to grow remiss in piety. When they have been quickened in a duty, they are apt to grow dead again. When they have been heated at the fire of an ordinance, they are apt to freeze again; therefore they still must be offering violence. The heart, like the watch, will be apt to run down; therefore it must be continually wound up by prayer and meditation. The fire of devotion will soon go out if it is not blown up.

A Christian's own experience of his inconstancy in performing good, is reason enough to holy violence.

If there must be this offering of violence, it shows us it is not so easy a thing as men imagine to get to Heaven. There are so many precepts to obey; so many promises to believe; so many rocks to avoid, that it is a difficult matter to be saved. Some imagine that there is a pleasant, easy way to Heaven—an idle wish, a deathbed tear—but the text tells us of offering violence. Alas, there is a great work to be done; the bias of the heart must be changed. Man by nature does not only lack grace—but hate it. He has an envenomed spirit against God, and is angry with converting grace; and is it easy to have the heart metamorphosed? for the proud heart to be made humble? for the earthly heart to be made heavenly? Can this be done without using violence? It is all up hill to Heaven, and it will make us sweat before we get to the top of the hill.

"Enter through the narrow gate. For wide is the gate and broad is the road that leads to destruction, and many enter through it. But small is the gate and narrow the road that leads to life, and only a few find it." Matthew 7:13-14. Indeed hell will be taken without storm: the gates of hell, like that iron gate, Acts xii. 10. open of their own accord; but if we get to Heaven, we must force our way; we must besiege it with sighs and tears, and get the scaling ladder of faith to storm it.

We must not only *work*—but *fight*. Like those Jews who built the wall of Jerusalem, Nehem. 4:17-18. "Those who carried materials did their *work* with one hand and held a *weapon* in the other, and each of the builders wore his *sword* at his side as he *worked*." A Christian is commanded to difficult service; he must charge through the whole army of his lusts, every one of which is stronger than Goliath. A Christian has no time to drowse; he must be either praying or watching; either upon the mount or in the valley, on the mount of faith or in the valley of humility.

Worldly things are not obtained without labor. What toiling is there in the shop? What sweatings are there in the furnace? And do we think Heaven will be had without labor? Do men dig for worms, and not for gold? Those who are *in* Heaven are employed; much more should those who are getting there. The angels are ministering spirits, Heb. i. 14. The wings of the seraphim are many—to show us how swift they are in God's service. If the angels in Heaven are busying themselves in noble and honorable employment, how industrious should we be who are getting up the hill of God, and have not yet arrived at a state of glory? Is salvation-work so easy? Can a man be saved by a faint wish? Can he leap out of the Devil's arms into Abraham's bosom? Oh no! there must be offering violence.

Some think free grace will save them; but it must be in the use of means. "Watch and pray." Others say, the promises will bring them to Heaven—but the promises of the Word are not to be separated from the precepts. The promise tells us of a crown—but the precept says, "Run in such a way as to get the prize," 1 Cor. 9:24. The promises are made to encourage faith, not to nourish sloth. But others say, Christ has died for sinners; and so they leave him to do all for them and they will do nothing. Then the text would be out of date, and all the exhortations to striving and "fighting the good fight of faith," are in vain. Our salvation cost Christ blood; it will cost us sweat. The boat may as well get to shore without rowing, as we can get to Heaven without offering violence.

2. It shows us the great mistake of ignorant people, who think the bare doing of duties, though in an ever so slight and superficial manner, is enough. The text tells us of offering violence,

1. In the business of **PRAYER**. They think it is enough to utter over a few words though the heart be asleep all the while. What offering of violence is here? Christ was "in an agony" at prayer, Luke xxii. 44. Many when they pray, are rather in a lethargy than in an agony. Jacob *wrestled* with the angel in prayer, Gen. xxxii. 24. The incense was to be laid upon *burning* coals, Lev. xvi. 12. Incense was a type of prayer and incense upon *burning* coals was a type of fervency in prayer. Few know what the spirit of prayer means; or what it is to have the affections boil over. When they are about the world they are all fire; when they are at prayer they are all ice.

2. In the **HEARING OF THE WORD**. Many people think it is enough to bring their *bodies* to the assembly—but never look at their *hearts*. They satisfy themselves that they have been at church, though they have not been with God, while there. Others go to a sermon as to the market—to hear the latest news. New notions please their fancy—but they do not attend to the Word as a matter of life and death. They do not go to meet with Christ in an ordinance; to have the breathings of his Spirit, and the infusions of his love. Alas, what little violence for Heaven is to be seen in most people's worship! In all the sacrifices of the law, there was *fire*. How can those duties be accepted which have no fire in them, no offering of violence.

3. If there must be this offering of violence to Heaven, then it shows us how dangerous *moderation in piety* is. Violence and moderation are two different things. Indeed, moderation in the things of the world is commendable. We should moderate our worldly desires—and "use the world as if we used it not," 1 Cor. vii. 31. We may, as Jonathan, dip the end of the rod in honey—but not thrust it in too far. In this sense moderation is good—but moderation in matters of practical piety is sinful—it is contrary to offering violence. Moderation, in the world's sense, means not to be too zealous, not to be too fierce for Heaven. Moderation is not to venture further in piety, than may coexist with self-preservation. As the king of Navarr told Beza—he would launch no farther into the sea than he might be sure to return safely to land. To keep on the *warm side of the hedge*, is a main article in the politicians creed.

Moderation in the world's sense, is neutrality. The moderate person finds a medium between strictness and profaneness; he is not for debauchery, nor for purity. It was the advice Calvin gave Melanchthon, that he should not so affect the name of moderate, that at last he lost all his zeal. To be lukewarm in matters of piety, is far from offering violence to Heaven, Rev iii. 19. "Be zealous and repent." If any should ask us why we are so violent, tell them it is for a kingdom. If any shall ask us why we make such haste in the ways of piety, tell them we are running a heavenly race, and a softly moderate pace will never win the prize. Moderation has made many lose Heaven; they have not made haste enough; they have come too late, (like the foolish virgins) when the door has been shut!

Reproofs to those not putting forth holy violence

"The Kingdom of Heaven suffers violence, and
the violent take it by force." Matthew 11:12

**Out of this text, I may draw forth
several arrows of REPROOF**

1. It reproves SLOTHFUL professors who are settled on their lees. They make a lazy profession of piety—but use no violence. They are like the lilies, which neither toil, nor do they spin. The snail, by reason of its slow motion, was reckoned among the unclean, Levit. xi. 30. St. Augustine calls idleness the burial of a man alive. There are some faint wishes, "oh that I had Heaven!" but a man may desire venison, and lack it, if he does not hunt for it. "The sluggard craves and gets nothing, but the desires of the diligent are fully satisfied." Proverbs 13:4

Men would be content to have the kingdom of Heaven; but they are loath to fight for it. They choose rather to go in a feather bed to Hell than to be carried to Heaven in a "fiery chariot" of zeal and violence. How many sleep away, and play away, their time; as if they were made like the Leviathan, to play in the sea! Psalm civ. 26. It is a saying of Seneca, "No man is made wise by chance." Sure it is, no man is saved by chance—but he must know how he came by it, namely, by offering violence. Such as have accustomed themselves to an idle, lazy disposition, will find it hard to shake off, "I have taken off my robe—must I put it on again? I have washed my feet-- must I soil them again?" Song of Songs 5:3. The spouse had laid herself upon the bed of sloth, and though Christ knocked at the door, she was reluctant to rise and let him in.

Some pretend to be believers—but are idle in the vineyard. They pretend to make use of faith for seeing—but not for working; this faith is fancy. O that Christians had a spirit of activity in them, 1 Chron. xxii. 16. "Arise and be doing, and the Lord be with you." We may sometimes learn of our enemy.

The **Devil** is never idle; he "walks about," 1 Peter v. 8. The world is his diocese and he is every day going on his visitation. Is Satan active? Is the enemy upon his march, coming against us? And are we asleep upon our guard? As Satan himself is not idle, so he will not endure that any of his servants should be idle. When the Devil had entered into Judas, how active was Judas! He goes to the high priest, from thence to the band of soldiers and with them back to the garden, and never left until he had betrayed Christ. Satan will not endure an idle servant; and do we think God will? How will the heathen rise up in judgment against slothful Christians!

What pains did they take in the **Olympian games**: they ran for a garland of flowers, and do we stand still who run for a crown of immortality? Certainly, if only the violent take Heaven, the idle person will never come there. God puts no difference between these two, slothful and wicked, Matt. xxv. 26."You *wicked* and *slothful* servant."

2. It reproves the FORMALIST, who puts all his religion in gestures and vestures, and emblems of devotion, and thinks this will entitle him to Heaven, Rev. iii. 1. "You have a name to live, and are dead." The form and outside of Christianity is judged as all that is necessary.

1. It is a means to keep up men's credit in the world. Should they be visibly profane, such as are sober would not come near them: they would be looked upon as no better than baptized heathens; therefore they must make a show of devotion out of policy, to gain some reputation and esteem among others.

2. A form serves to stop the mouth of conscience; had they not some kind of outward devotion, their conscience would fly in their face and they would be a terror to themselves; therefore they think it expedient to have a form of godliness. But alas! what is all this? The text speaks of offering violence to heaven. What violence is there in a form? Here is no taking pains with the heart: a form—but no power, 2 Tim. iii. 5. Formalists are like the statues in the churchyard, which have their eyes and hands lifted up to Heaven—but have no soul. The formalist's devotion runs out most in punctilios and niceties: he neglects "the weightier matters of the law, faith and mercy," Matt. xxiii. 23. He scruples about superstitious fancies—but makes no reckoning of sin: he is more afraid of a black cat crossing his path, than of a harlot in his bed. He hates sanctity. Christ had no such bitter enemies as the formal pharisees. The formalist is never violent—but in persecuting the power of godliness.

3. It reproves such as are violent in a bad sense. They are violent for hell; they go there in the sweat of their brows. Jer 8:6, "Each pursues his own course like a horse charging into battle." A war horse rushes violently among the guns and cannons: so did they rush into sin violently. Men are violent,

1. In opposing good.

2. In pursuing evil.

1. Men are violent in opposing good. Several ways.

1. They offer violence to the Spirit of God. The Spirit knocks at the door of sinners" hearts; he waits until his head is "filled with dew," and "his locks with the drops of the night;" but sinners repulse and grieve the Spirit, and send away this dove from the ark of their souls. Acts vii. 51. "You do always resist the Holy Spirit." The Spirit offers grace to the sinner, and the sinner offers violence to the Spirit, Isaiah lxiii. 10. "They rebelled and vexed His Holy Spirit;" and may not the Lord give up striving. God, who is willing to come in when we open to him, has not promised to come again if we unkindly repulse Him.

2. They offer violence to conscience. Conscience is God's preacher in the heart. This preacher cannot flatter; it tells men of their pride, covetousness, abuse of mercy. But they, instead of being violent against their sins, offer violence to conscience; they silence and imprison conscience. But as the prophet Zachariah when he was dumb, called for a writing table and did write, Luke i. 63. So when conscience cannot be permitted to speak, it will write. It writes down men's sins; and when at death they shall be forced to read the hand-writing, it will make their hearts tremble, and their knees knock together. Men commonly offer violence to their conscience; and what will be this outcome? Those who will not hear the *voice* of conscience, shall be sure to feel the *worm* of conscience!

3. They offer violence to God's image. The saints (who are God's living picture) are opposed and shot at. This is a cursed violence, Gal. iv. 29. "As he who was born after the flesh, persecuted him who was born after the Spirit;" even so it is now. Christ himself is struck at through believers. The church has always been in the torrid zone—the ploughers have ploughed upon her back. The earth has been sown with the bodies of the saints, and watered with their blood. Persecutors, I grant, are of an ancient family. The first man that was born in the world was a persecutor, namely Cain; and he has a numerous offspring: Nero, Trajan, Domitian, Diocletian, and Maximinus. Faelix, earl of Wurtemburg, being at supper in Augsburg, did take an oath that before he died, he would ride up to the spurs in the blood of the Lutherans; but was afterwards choked in his own blood. Persecutors are the curse of the creation: being some of those "thorns and briars" which the earth brings forth.

2. Men are violent in pursuing evil.

1. They are violent in their **opinions**. 2 Peter ii. 1. "Privily they shall bring in damnable heresies." Arius was such a one; and truly the spirit of Arius is yet alive at this day, when men dare deny the Deity of the blessed Son of God. Many of the

heretics of old were so violent, that their opinion was to them a Bible: and some of them died maintaining their heresies. These were the Devil's martyrs.

2. They are violent in their **passions**. Anger is a temporary insanity, James iii. 6. "The tongue is a fire, a world of iniquity." In this little member there is a great world, namely, a "world of sin." Such as would be counted sober—yet are drunk with passion. Their prayers, are cold—but their anger hot. They spit fire as the serpent does poison. Fiery passions, without repentance, bring men to the fiery furnace.

3. They are violent for their **lusts**. Titus 3:3. "Enslaved by all kinds of passions and pleasures." Lust is an inordinate desire or impulse, provoking the soul to the gratifying of its carnal desires. Aristotle calls them brutish lusts, because when lusts are violent, they will not let reason or conscience be heard; but a man is carried brutishly to the satisfying of the flesh.

1. Men are violent for their *drunken* lusts. Though death is in the cup, they will drink it up. One having almost lost his eye-sight, the physician told him there was no cure for him, unless he would leave off his excessive drinking. "Then," says he, "farewell sweet light!" He would rather lose his eye-sight than leave his drinking.

2. They are violent for their *impure* lusts. Men are said to "burn in lusts," Romans i. 27. The apostle intimates that lust is a kind of fever. Feverish heats are not more pernicious to the body, than lust is to the soul. O what folly is it—for a drop of pleasure to drink a sea of wrath!

3. They are violent for their *oppressive* lusts, who wrong and defraud others, and by violence take away their right. Instead of clothing the naked, they make those who are clothed, naked. These *birds of prey* live upon rapine. They are cruel, as if they had been suckled with the milk of wolves. They smile at the curses of the poor, and grow fat with their tears. They have forgotten Christ's caveat, Luke iii. 14. "Do violence to no man." Ahab violently took away Naboth's vineyard, 2 Kings xxi. 11. Hell is taken by this violence, Proverbs iv. 17. "Who drink the wine of violence." This wine will turn to poison at last, Psalm. xi. 5, "He who loves violence, God's soul hates."

4. They are violent for their *covetous* lusts. Covetousness is the soul's idolatry. Amos 2:7, "Who pant after the dust of the earth." They compass sea and land to make money their proselyte. Their God is made of gold, and to it they bow down. Those who bowed down on their knees to drink of the waters, were accounted unfit soldiers for Gideon, Judges vii. 6. So are those unfit for Christ, that stoop immoderately to the care of earthly things. Those who are violent for the world, what have they but the wind? Eccles. v. 16. "What profit has he who has labored for the wind?" The world cannot enrich the soul, it cannot remove pain. If pangs of conscience come, the world

can no more give comfort, than a crown of gold can cure a head-ache.

4. It reproves those who have in part left off that holy strictness and violence in piety they once had. Their fervor is cooled and abated. What they do is so little, that it cannot be called violence. They serve God—but are not fervent in spirit. They do not abandon duty—but they grow dead in duty. They have "left their first love," Rev. ii. 4. It is with them as a fire when it is going out; or as the sun when it is going down. Like epileptics, before they were in a paroxysm, or hot fit of zeal; but now that the cold fit has taken them, they are formal and frozen in piety. Time was when they called "the Sabbath a delight," Isaiah. lviii. 13. How were their hearts raised in duty! How diligently did they seek him whom their soul loved! But now the case is altered; their piety languishes, and even vanishes. Time was when they were in an agony, and did send forth strong cries in prayer. Now the chariot wheels are pulled off, and the spirit of prayer is much abated. Their prayers freeze between their lips; a clear sign of the decay of grace. These persons are grown both *lethargic* and *consumptive*.

1. *Lethargic.* Cant. v. 2, "I sleep—but my heart wakes" Though grace was alive in her, and her heart waked; yet she was in a dull, drowsy temper, "I sleep." When the heart burns in sin, and cools in duty, it is a sure sign of growing to a stupid lethargy.

2. *Consumptive.* There are two signs of persons in a spiritual consumption.

1. When their desire after Christ and Heaven is not as strong as it was. A consumptive man's stomach decays. Christians have not such violent affections to heavenly things; they can desire food and wine, and the luscious delights of the earth; but Christ is less precious; they are not in pangs of desire after him; a sad symptom their grace is in a consumption.

2. When they are not so vigorous in motion. When a man is lively and stirring at his work—it is a sign he is in health. But when he is listless, and does not care to stir, or put his hand to anything—it is a sign that health is declining. So when men have no heart for that which is holy, they care not to put themselves upon the exercises of piety; they have lost a spirit of activity for God; they serve him in a faint sickly manner. It is is a sign they are consumptive.

When the pulse can scarcely be felt, and it beats very low, men are near dying. So when those who were once violent for heaven—but now we can scarce perceive any godliness in them, the pulse beats low—and grace is ready to die, Rev. iii. 2.

To you who have abated in your holy violence, and are grown remiss in duty, let me expostulate with you, as the Lord did by the prophet, Jer. ii. 5. "What iniquity have your fathers found in me?"

What evil have you found in **God**, that you leave off your former strictness? Has not God fed you with manna from above, and given you his Holy Spirit to be your guide and comforter? Has he not made you swim in a sea of mercy?

What evil have you found in **prayer**, that you are less violent in it? Have you not had sweet fellowship with God? Have you not sometimes been melted and enlarged, insomuch you have thought yourselves in the suburbs of Heaven, when you have been upon this mount? Has not the dove of prayer brought an olive-branch of peace in its mouth?

What evil have you found in the **Word**? Time was when you did take this book and eat it—and it was honey in your mouth! Has the Word less virtue in it now? Are the promises like Aaron's dry rod, withered and sapless?

What iniquity have you found in the **ways of God**, that you have abated your former violence in piety? "O remember whence you are fallen, and repent, and do your first works," Rev. ii. 5.

Consider seriously—

1. The less violence for heaven, the less peace you will have. Our consciences are never at peace in a drowsy state. It is the lively acting of grace, which makes the heart calm and serene. These two go together, walking "in the fear of God,"and "in the comforts of the Holy Spirit," Acts ix. 31. Christian, if once you grow remiss in piety, conscience will chide you. If you belong to God, he will never let you be quiet—but will send some affliction or other to awaken you out of your security, and make you recover that active lively frame of heart as once you had.

2. You who grow more dead in God's service, and leave your first love—give great advantage to Satan. The less violent you are—the more violent he is. The less you pray—the more he tempts. What a sad case are you now in? How can grace that is weak and sickly withstand violent temptations? Hence it is God allows his own people sometimes to fall into sin, as a just punishment for their lukewarmness, and to make them more zealous and violent for the future.

3. Your remissness in piety, though it may not damn you—it will damage you. You will lose that degree of glory, which else you might have had. Though your remissness may not lose your crown, it will lessen it and make it weigh lighter.

4. The more lazy a Christian's desires are, the more lively his corruptions. The weaker the body grows, the stronger the disease grows. O, therefore, pray for quickening grace, Psalm cxliii. 11. Beg for fresh gales of the Spirit to blow upon you. Never leave until you have recovered that holy violence which once you had.

2. It reproves those who have nearly abandoned all violence—they have stopped reading and praying in their family. There is not so much as a face of piety to be seen; they are fallen finally. Such were Joash, Jehu, Julian. The goodly building of their profession, which others admired, now has not one stone left upon another.

WHY do men thus run retrograde in their motion, and quite throw off that violence which they seemed once to have?

1. Because they never had a principle of spiritual life. Things that move from a principle of life are constant, as the motion of the pulse. But artificial things are apt to be at a stand-still, and their motion ceases. As a clock when the weights are hung on, goes—but take off the weights and it stands still. So the apostate never moved in religion, but for gain and applause. When these weights are taken off, he is at a stand-still, he goes no further. That branch must needs wither, which has no root to grow upon.

2. Men throw off all violence, and degenerate into apostasy, because they never did duties of piety with delight. Paul "delighted in the law of God in the inward man, Romans vii. 22. It was his Heaven to serve God. A man who delights in pleasure will never give up his pleasure. The apostate never had any true delight in the ways of God; he was rather forced with fear, than drawn with love; he served a master whom he never cared for; no wonder then that he leaves his service.

3. Men degenerate into apostasy through unbelief. Psalm lxxviii. 22. "They believed not in God." verse 41. "They turned back, and tempted God." Sinners have jealous thoughts of God; they distrust his love, therefore desert his service. They think they may pray, and hear—and to no purpose. Mal. iii. 14. "What profit is it that we have kept his ordinances?" That is, "We may draw near to God in duty—but he will never draw near to us in mercy." Thus unbelief and atheism prevailing, the livery of piety is presently thrown off, and all former violence for Heaven ceases. Unbelief is the mother of apostasy.

4. Men leave off their former violence, and prove to be Judases and Devils, because they love something else more than piety. There is some lust or other, that their heart is engaged to; and their violence for sin has destroyed their violence for piety. Solyman, the great Turk, seeing many professing Christians go over to Turkism, he asked them what moved them to turn Turks. They replied, "they did it to be eased of their taxes." They were drawn from God through the prevalency of covetousness. If there is any predominant, lust in the heart—it will get domination, and destroy all former zeal for piety. Abimelech, a bastard, destroyed "seventy of his brethren upon one stone," Judges ix. 18. If there is any lust the heart runs after, this bastard-sin will destroy seventy duties; it will murder all that violence for Heaven, which a man did once seem to have.

5. Men leave off former violence out of cowardice. If they are violent in piety, they fear they may lose their profits and preferments; nay, even their lives. The coward never yet won the field. When carnal fear grows violent—all violence for Heaven is at an end.

Many of the Jews who were great followers of Christ, when they saw the swords and staves, left him. (Proverbs xxix. 25. "In the fear of man there is a snare." Carnal fear makes the *sin* appear less than it is—but the *danger* greater.

6. Men leave off violence for Heaven—for lack of patience. Sensible feeling of joy is withheld, and they have no patience to stay for the full recompense of reward. Hypocrites are all for present pay; and if they have not that suddenly which they desire, they bid adieu to piety; and say as that wicked king, 2 Kings vi. 33. "Why should I wait for the Lord any longer?" They do not consider that God is a free agent, and will dispense his blessings in the fittest season—but they try to tie God up to their time. They forget that joy is a part of the reward; and would have the reward, before their work not yet finished. Does the servant receive his pay before his work is done? James v. 6. "The farmer waits for the precious fruit of the earth." He does not expect to sow and reap in the same day. But hypocrites are always in haste: they would reap joy before they are done sowing the seed of repentance. And because comfort is a while deferred, they are offended; they will serve God no longer; their patience is at an end, therefore their violence is at an end.

7. Men leave off holy violence, and degenerate into profaneness, out of a just judgment from God, leaving them to themselves. They often resisted the Spirit, and sent him away sad. And now, as a just judgment, God says, "my Spirit shall no longer strive." And if this wind does not blow upon their sails, they cannot move. If this sun withdraws from their climate, they must needs freeze in impenitency. They before sinned against clear convictions; they silenced conscience—and now God has seared it. And now if an angel should preach to them from Heaven, it would do them no good. O how dismal is this! the thoughts of it may strike us into a holy consternation.

Thus we see **why** men apostatize and leave off their violence for Heaven.

What do they get by this? Let us see what a purchase apostates make.

They proclaim their FOLLY. For all their former violence for Heaven is lost. He who runs half the race and then faints, loses the garland. Ezek. xniii. 24. "When the righteous turns away from his righteousness, all his righteousness that he has done shall not be mentioned." All men's prayers and tears are lost. The apostate unravels all that he has been doing. He is like a man who with a pencil draws an intricate picture, and then comes with his sponge and wipes it out again. Gal. iii. 4. "Have you suffered so many things in vain?" Perhaps for piety, a man has suffered many a reproach and affront; and have you suffered all this in vain? Here is folly indeed.

It will be BITTERNESS in the end. Jer. ii. 19. "Know therefore that it is an **evil** and **bitter** thing that you have forsaken the Lord." Men, by leaving off their violence for Heaven, get a thorn in their *conscience*, a blot in their *name*, a curse in their *souls*. What did Judas get by his apostasy—but a halter? So it will be bitterness in the end. The apostate, when he dies, drops as a windfall into the devil's mouth!

5. It reproves those who put off this violence for the kingdom, until old age. When they are fit for no other work, then they will begin this taking heaven by storm. No man says, "I will learn my trade when I am old." It is imprudence for one to begin to work for Heaven, when he is past his labor. There is a night of sickness and death coming, and our Savior says, "The night comes when no man can work," John ix. 4. Surely a man can put forth but little violence for Heaven when old age, and old sins are upon him. Besides, how unworthy and insincere it is--to give the Devil the *flower of youth*, and God the *dregs of old age!* Therefore God rejected Cain's sacrifice, because it was stale before he brought it, Gen. iv. 3. There is little hope of their salvation--who are never seek for Heaven, until they are on the borders of eternity.

6. It reproves those who are so far from using this violence for Heaven, that they deride it. These are your zealous ones, 2 Peter iii. 3. "In the last days there shall be scoffers." Holy walking has become the object of derision. Psalm lxix. 12. "I have become the song of the drunkard." This shows a vile heart. There are some, who, though they have no goodness themselves—yet honor those who are good. Herod reverenced John the Baptist. But what devils are those—who scoff at goodness, and reproach others for doing that which God commands. This age produces such as sit in the chair of scorners, and throw their squibs at piety. In Bohemia, when some of the martyrs were the next day to suffer, they comforted themselves with this—that was their last supper and tomorrow they should feast with Christ in Heaven! A Papist standing by, asked them in a jeer—if Christ had any cooks in Heaven to dress their supper? Oh, take heed of such an Ishmael spirit! It is a sign of a man given over to the devil. God 'scorns the scorner" Proverbs iii. 34. And surely, he shall never live with

God whose company God scorns.

7. It reproves those who instead of taking Heaven by force, keep it off by force; as if they were afraid of being happy; or as if a crown of glory would hurt them. Such are,

1. The **ignorant**, who shut their eyes against the light, and refuse to be taught the way to Heaven. Hosea iv. 6. "You have rejected knowledge." The Hebrew word shoves to reject with disdain. As I have read of a Scotch bishop, who thanked God he never knew what the old and new Testaments were. I wonder where the bishop took his text.

2. The **profane**, who hate to be admonished, and had rather die than reform. Amos v. 10. "They hate him who rebukes in the gate." These keep off heaven by force. Such were those in Acts xiii. 46. "Seeing you put away the Word from you." The Greek word may be rendered, seeing you shove it away with your shoulders. As if a sick man should bolt out the physician, lest he should cure him. Job xxi. 14. "Who say unto the Almighty, depart from us!" God is reluctant to be gone; he woos and beseeches sinners to accept his terms of mercy—but sinners will have him gone; they say to him "Depart!" May not we say to these, "who has bewitched you? What madness beyond hyperbole is this—that you should not only forsake mercy—but fight against it; as if there were danger in going to Heaven!"

These who put away salvation from them, they do willfully perish; they would not hear of anything that would save them. Were it not be a sad epitaph if a man had written upon his tomb-stone, "here lies one who murdered himself"? This is the condition of desperate sinners; they keep off Heaven by force; they are self murderers. Therefore God writes their epitaph upon their grave, Hosea xiii. 9. "O Israel—you have destroyed yourself!"

Examination and Objections

Let us then **EXAMINE** whether we put forth this holy violence for Heaven? What is an empty profession without this? It is Like a lamp without oil. Let us all ask ourselves—what violence do we use for Heaven?

1. Do we strive with our hearts to get them into a holy frame? How did David awaken all the powers of his soul to serve God, Psalm 87:6. "I myself will awake early."

2. Do we set time apart to call ourselves to account, and to try our evidences for Heaven? Psalm lxxxvii. 6. "My spirit made diligent search." Do we take our hearts as a watch all in pieces, to see what is amiss and to mend it? Are we meticulously inquisitive into the state of our souls? Are we afraid of artificial grace, as of artificial happiness?

3. Do we use violence in prayer? Is there fire in our sacrifice? Does the wind of the Spirit, filling our sails, cause "groans unutterable?" Romans viii. 25. Do we pray in the morning as if we were to die at night?

4. Do we thirst for the living God? Are our souls big with holy desires? Psalm lxxiii. 25. "There is none upon earth that I desire beside you." Do were desire holiness as well as Heaven? Do we desire as much to look like Christ, as to live with Christ? Is our desire constant? Is this spiritual pulse always beating?

5. Are we skilled in self-denial? Can we deny our ease, our aims, our interest? Can we cross our own will to fulfill God's? Can we behead our beloved sin? To pluck out the right eye requires violence.

6. Are we lovers of God? It is not how much we *do*—but how much we *love*. Does love command the castle of our hearts? Does Christ's beauty and sweetness constrain us? 2 Cor. v. 14. Do we love God more than we fear hell?

7. Do we keep our spiritual watch? Do we set spies in every place, watching our thoughts, our eyes, our tongues? When we have prayed against sin, do we watch against temptation? The Jews, having sealed the stone of Christ's sepulcher, 'set a watch," Matt. xxvii. 66. After we have been at the Word, do we set a watch?

8. Do we press after further degrees of sanctity? Phil iii. 13. "Reaching forth unto those things which are before." A godly Christian is a wonder; he is the most contented yet the least satisfied: he is contented with a little of the world—but not satisfied with a little grace; he would have still more faith and be anointed with fresh oil. Paul desired to "attain unto the resurrection of the dead," Phil. iii. 11, that is, he endeavored (if possible) to arrive at such a measure of grace as the saints shall have at the resurrection.

9. Is there a holy emulation in us? Do we labor to out-shine others in piety? To be more eminent for love and good works? Do we something which is singular? Matt. v. 47. "What do you do, more than others?"

10. Are we got above the world? Though we walk on earth, do we trade in Heaven? Can we say as David? Psalm cxxxxix. 17. "I am still with you." This requires violence; for motions upward are usually violent.

11. Do we set ourselves always under God's eye? Psalm xvi. 8. "I have set the Lord always before me." Do we live soberly and godly, remembering that whatever we are doing our Judge looks on?

If it be thus with us, we are happy people. This is the holy violence the text speaks of, and is the right way of taking the kingdom of God. And surely never did Noah so willingly put forth his hand to receive the dove into the ark, as Jesus Christ will put forth His hand to receive us into Heaven.

Before I press the exhortation, let me remove some **OBJECTIONS** that may be made against this blessed violence.

1. But we have no power of ourselves to save ourselves? You bid us be violent, as if you should bid a man chained fast in fetters to walk.

It is true, we cannot, until grace comes, effectually operate to our own salvation. Before conversion we are purely passive; and when God bids us convert and turn, this is to show us what we ought to do, not what we can do. Yet let us do what we are able.

We have power to avoid those rocks, which will certainly ruin our souls—I mean gross sins. A man does not need to be in bad company; he does not need to swear, or tell lies; nor would he do it if it were by law death to swear an oath.

We have power to cast ourselves upon the use of means, praying, reading, holy conference. This will condemn men at the last day; that they did not act so vigorously in their sphere as they might; they did not use the means, and see whether God will give grace. God will come with that soliciting question at last, "You should have put my money on deposit with the bankers, so that when I returned I would have received it back with interest." Mat. 25:27. "Why did you not improve that power which I gave you?"

Though we do not have power to save ourselves—yet we must pursue after salvation, because God has made a promise of grace, as well as to grace. He has promised to circumcise our hearts; to put his Spirit within us; to enable us to walk in his statutes, Ezek. xxxvi. 27. So that by prayer we are to put the bond in suit, and to press God with his own promise. Though I will not say with the Arminians, that upon our endeavor God is bound to give grace; yet he is not lacking to those who seek his grace; nay, he denies his grace to none but those who willfully refuse it, Psalm lxxxi. 11, "Israel would have none of me."

2. But this offering violence is HARD, and I shall never be able to go through it.

Admit it to be hard—yet it is a duty, and there is no disputing duty. God has made the way to Heaven hard.

To try our obedience. A child obeys his father, though he commands him hard things. Peter's obedience and love was tried when Christ bade him come to him upon the water.

God does it that he may raise the price of heavenly things. Were the kingdom of glory easily obtained, we would not value its worth. Such is our nature, that we slight things which are easily come by. If pearls were common, they would soon fall in their price. If Christ and Heaven might be had without violence, these blessings of the first magnitude would not have been had in such high veneration.

But let not the difficulty be objected. What if salvation-work is hard.

1. Is it not harder to lay in Hell? Is not suffering vengeance worse than offering violence?

2. We do not argue so in other things. An estate is hard to come by; therefore we will sit still? No! difficulty does the more whet and sharpen our endeavor; and if we take such pains for these inferior things, how should we for that which is more noble and sublime! The profit will abundantly countervail the labor.

3. Though the business of piety at first seems hard—yet when once we are entered into it, it is pleasant. When the wheels of the soul are oiled with grace, now a Christian moves in piety with facility and delight, Romans vii. 22. "I delight in the law of God after the inward man." Christ's yoke at the first putting on seems heavy; but when once it is on, it is easy. To serve God, to love God, to enjoy God, is the sweetest freedom in the world. The poets say the top of Olympus is always quiet. The first climbing up the rocky hill of Heaven is hard to flesh and blood; but when we are gotten up towards the top, there is peace and delight; we see a pleasant prospect, and are ready to cry out as Peter on the mount of transfiguration, "It is good to be here!" What hidden manna do we now find! This is the anticipation or foretaste of glory.

3. But if I put myself upon this violent exercise in piety, then I shall lose that pleasure I have in my sin, my mirth and melody, and I shall exchange delight for labor; and so I shall be no more Naomi—but Marah. Voluptuous people speak as the fig tree in the parable, Judges ix. "Shall I leave my fatness and sweetness," all my former pleasures, and now offer violence to Heaven, live a strict mortified life? This crosses the stream of corrupt nature.

Leave the pleasure in sin. The Scripture does so describe sin, that one would think there should be little pleasure in it.

1. Scripture calls sin a **debt**. Sin is compared to a debt of "ten thousand talents" Matt. xviii. 24. A talent of gold among the Hebrews, was valued at almost four thousand pounds. Ten thousand talents is a figurative speech, to express how great a debt sin is; and do you call this a pleasure? Is it any pleasure for a man to be in debt?

2. Scripture calls sin a **disease**, Isaiah i. 5. "The whole head is sick." Is it any pleasure to be sick? Though all do not feel this sickness—yet the less the distemper is felt, the more deadly it is.

3. The Scripture compares sin to "**gall** and **wormwood**," Deut. xxix. 18. It breeds a bitter worm in the conscience. Sin stings a man with wrath, John iii. 34. And do you call this a pleasure? Surely, you "put bitter for sweet," Isaiah v, 20.

The pleasures of sin gratify only the senses of man, and are not soul. Pleasures are called carnal, because they delight only the body. How absurd was that speech of the rich man in the Gospel, when he was speaking of his store of goods and his barns being full, 'soul, take your ease," Luke xii.19. He might have said more properly, "body, take your ease;" for his soul was never the better for his riches, nor could it feel any delight in them. Though his barns were full, his soul was empty. Therefore, when Satan tell you, "if you use violence for Heaven, you will lose all your pleasures;" ask him, "what pleasures are they, Satan? such as please only the senses, they do not delight the mind; they do not comfort the conscience; they are such delights wherein the brute creatures do exceed me!"

These sugared pleasures in sin the Scripture says are but "for a season," Heb. xi. 25. They are like straw in a fire—which makes a blaze—but is presently out. 1 John ii. 17. "The world passes away, and the lust thereof." It passes away swiftly as a ship under sail. **Worldly pleasures perish in the using**; like a fleeting shadow or flash of lightning; and are these to be preferred before an eternal weight of glory?

The present sweetness which is in sin will turn to bitterness at last. Like the book the prophet ate, Ezek. iii. 3, sweet in the mouth—but bitter in the belly. Honey is sweet—but it turns to nausea. Sin is a sweet poison, it delights the palate—but torments the soul. When once the sinner's eyes come to be opened at death, and he feels some sparks of God's wrath in his conscience, then he will cry out in horror, and be ready to lay violent hands upon himself. We may say of the pleasures of sin, as Solomon says of wine, Prov xxiii. 32. "Afterwords it bites like a serpent." So look not on the smiling pleasures of sin; be not delighted with its beauty—but affrighted of its sting! Do the damned in Hell feel any pleasure now in their sins? Has their cup of wrath have one drop of honey in it? Oh remember, after the golden crowns, and women's hair—come the lions teeth! Rev. iv. 8. Thus I have answered the first part of the objection; I shall lose all my pleasures in sin.

If I put forth this violence in piety, I shall exchange my delight for labor. I must dig away through the rock, and while I work I must weep."

Though you must use violence—yet it is a sweet violence; it is a labor turned into delight. Psalm cxxxviii. 5. "They shall sing in the ways of the Lord." To send out faith as a spy to view the heavenly Canaan, and pluck a bunch of grapes there—this is great delight! Rom xv. 13. "Joy in believing." To love God, (in whom all excellencies are combined) how sweet is this! To love beauty is delightful. To walk among the promises as among beds of spices and to taste the fruit, oh how pleasant is this! The labor of a Christian brings peace of conscience, and joy in the Holy Spirit.

And whereas it is said that this holy violence takes away our joy, and while we work we must weep; I answer, a Christian would not be without these tears. **The tears of a saint** (says Bernard) **have more true joy in them than all worldly delights!** The oil of joy is for mourners, Isaiah lxi. 3.

4. I would use this violence for Heaven—but I shall expose myself to the censure and scorn of others. They will wonder to see me so altered, and think it nothing but a religious frenzy.

1. Consider **who** will reproach you; they are the wicked! They are such if Christ were alive on earth, would reproach him. They are blinded by the Satan, the god of this world, 2 Cor. iv. 4. It is as if a blind man should reproach a beautiful face!

2. **What** do they reproach you for? It is for offering violence to Heaven. Is it a disgrace, to be laboring for a kingdom? Tell them you are doing the work which God has set the about. Better they should reproach you for working in the vineyard—than God damn you for not working!

3. Jesus Christ was reproached for your sake, Heb xii. 2. "He endured the shame of the cross;" and will not you be contented to bear reproaches for him? These are but the *chips* of the cross, which are rather to be despised than laid to heart.

5. If I use this holy violence, and turn religious, then I shall lose such yearly profits which my sin has brought in. As Amaziah said, "But what about the hundred talents I paid for these Israelite troops?" 2 Chron. 25:9.

Is there any profit in sin? Did anyone ever thrive upon that trade? By the time you have cast up the reckoning, you will find but little profit.

1. By the incomes that sin brings in—you treasure up God's vengeance! Romans ii. 5. While you put unjust gain in the bag—God puts wrath in his vial! Will you call this profit? Whatever money a man gets in a sinful way—he must pay interest for it in hell!

2. That cannot be for your profit, which makes you come off a loser at last. You lose Heaven and your soul; and what can countervail this loss? "What is a man profited if he shall gain the whole world, and lose his own soul?" Matt. xvi. 26. "God" (says Chrysostom) "has given a man two eyes; if he loses one, he has another. But he has but one soul, and if that be lost—he is undone forever!"

6. But I have so much business in the world that I can find no time for this holy violence. As the king of Macedon said, when they presented him with a book treating of happiness, "I have no time for this!"

See the folly of this objection; what is the main business of life—but looking after the soul? And for men to say they are so immersed in the world, that they cannot mind their souls—is most absurd and irrational. This is to make the greater give way to the lesser. As if a farmer should say, he is so busy looking after his hobbies, that he has no time to plow or sow. What is his occupation but ploughing? Such madness is it to hear men say they are so taken up about the world that they have no time for their souls.

Could God find time to think of your salvation? Could Jesus Christ find time to come into the world, and be here thirty-three years in carrying on this great design of your redemption; and can you find no time to look after it? Is the getting a little money that which obstructs this violence for Heaven? Your money will perish with you!

Can you find time for your body? time to eat and sleep? and not find time for your soul? Can you find time to use for your *recreation?* and no time to use for your *salvation?* Can you find time for idle visits? and no time to visit the throne of grace?

Oh take heed that you go not to Hell in the crowd of worldly business! Joshua was a commander of an army—yet his work as a soldier was not to hinder his work as a Christian: he must pray as well as fight and take the book of the law in his hand, as well as the sword, Josh. i. 8.

You, whoever you are, who makes this objection about worldly business, let me ask you—do you think in your conscience, that this will be a good excuse at the last day, when God shall ask you, "Why did you not take pains for Heaven?" You shall say, "Lord, I was so steeped in worldly business, that I was hindered." Was it a good plea for a servant to say to his master, that he was so drunk that he could not work! Truly, it is a poor excuse to say that you "were so drunk with the cares of the world—that you could not be violent for the kingdom!"

27 Motives to put forth holy violence

Having answered these objections, let me reassume the exhortation, pressing all Christians to this violence for the heavenly kingdom. As David's three worthies ventured their lives, and broke through the army of the Philistines for water, 2 Sam. xxiii. 46, such a kind of violence must we use, breaking through all dangers for obtaining the "water of life."

1. Consider the *deplorable condition* we are in by nature—a state of misery and damnation; therefore what violence should we use to get out of it? Were one plunged into quicksands, would he not use violence to get out? Sin is a quicksand, and is it not wisdom to extricate ourselves out? David being encompassed with enemies, said "His soul was among lions," Psalm lvii. 4. It is true in a spiritual sense, our soul is among lions. Every sin is a lion which would devour us! And if we are in the lion's den—should not we use violence to get out? The angels used violence to Lot; they laid hold on him and pulled him out of Sodom, Gen. xix. 16. Such violence must be used to get out of the spiritual Sodom. It is not safe to stay in the enemy's quarters.

2. It is *possible* that in the use of means we may arrive at happiness. Impossibility destroys endeavor; but here is a door of hope opened. The thing is feasible. It is not with us as with the damned in hell; there is a tomb-stone rolled over them. But while we are under the sound of Aaron's bell, and the silver trumpet of the gospel is blown in our ears, while the spirit of grace breathes on us, and we are on this side of the grave—there is great hope that by holy violence we may win Paradise. An absolute impossibility of salvation is only for those who have committed the unpardonable sin against the Holy Spirit, and cannot repent; but who these are, is a secret sealed up in God's book. But here is great encouragement to all to be serious and earnest in the matters of eternity, because they are yet in a capacity of mercy, no final sentence is already passed; God has not yet taken up the *drawbridge of mercy*. Though the gate of Paradise is narrow—yet it is not shut. This should be as oil to the wheels, to make us lively and active in the business of salvation. Therefore as the farmer plows in hope, James v. so we should pray in hope; and do all our work for heaven in hope—for the *white flag of mercy* is yet held forth! So long as there was grain to be had in Egypt, the sons of Jacob would not sit starving at home, Gen. xliii. 3. So long as there is a kingdom to be obtained—let us not sit starving in our sins any longer!

3. This violence for Heaven is the grand business of our lives! What else did we come into the world for? We did not come here only to eat and drink, and wear fine clothes; but the end of our living is, to be violent for the kingdom of glory. Should the *body* only be tended, this were be to polish the scabbard, and let the blade rust; to preserve the lumber, and let the child be burnt. God sends us into the world as a merchant sends his goods to trade for him beyond the seas. So God sends us here to follow a spiritual trade, to serve him and save our souls. If we spend all our time in dressing and pampering our bodies, or idle visits—we shall give but a sad account to God, when he shall send us a letter of summons by death and bid us give an account of our stewardship!

Were not he much to be blamed, who would have a great deal of timber given him to build a house if he only cut all this good timber into chips? Just so is the case of many; God gives them precious **time** in which they are to provide for a kingdom, and they waste this time of life and cut it all into chips. Let this excite violence in the things of God. It is the main errand of our living here—and shall we go through the world and forget our errand?

4. How violent are the wicked in ways of sin! Violent for their malicious lusts! Proverbs i. 16. "Their feet run to evil." Violent for their unclean lusts. Amnon offered violence to his sister; he would have his lust, though it cost him his life. **Sinners tire themselves out in the devil's drudgery!** Jer. ix. 5. They "weary themselves to commit iniquity." They are out of breath in pursuing their sin! Jer. l. 33. "They are mad upon their idols!" So violent were the Jews, that they would spare no cost in their idolatrous worship, Isaiah xlvi. 6. "They lavish gold out of the bag." So fiercely were they bent upon idolatry, that they would sacrifice their sons and daughters to their idol gods, Jer. xxxii. 35. "They built the high places of Baal to cause their sons and their daughters to pass through the fire." Were men thus violent for their lusts and idols—and shall not we be violent for a kingdom?

Nay, you that are now ingrafted into Christ, how violent perhaps have some of you formerly been in evil? How did you once spend yourselves in a sinful way! Perhaps even like Paul, who before his conversion breathed out "threatenings and slaughter against the disciples of the Lord," Acts ix. 1. Perhaps you have been violent in drawing others to sin, you have been tempters to them; and perhaps some of them whom you have seduced to sin, are now crying because of you in hell, and saying that they would have never come there, if it had not been for your example! Should not the consideration of this humble you? Should not this make you the more violent in piety, that you may bring some glory to God before you die? Should you not be as industrious to save souls—as you have been to damn them? Were you to live to the age of Methuselah, you could never do God sufficient service for the dishonor you have done to him!

5. This holy violence has much delight mingled with it. Prov iii. 17. "All her ways are pleasantness" Though the way of piety has thorns in it, (in respect to persecution) yet it is full of roses, in respect to that inward peace and contentment that the soul finds in it. A man is violent at his recreation; but there is an inward delight he takes in it which sweetens that violence. Paul made **piety** his recreation. Rom vii. 22. "I delight in the law of God after the inward man." In the Greek, "I take pleasure." Not only Heaven itself is delightful—but the way there. What ravishing delight a gracious soul has in **prayer**? Isaiah lvi. 7. "I will make them joyful in the house of prayer." What delight in **holy contemplation!** A Christian has such influences of the Spirit, and meets with such transfigurations of soul, that he thinks himself half in heaven! Serving of God is like gathering spices, or flowers, wherein there is some labor—but the labor is recompensed with delight! The way of sin has bitterness in it. The bears, while they lick honey, are stung with the bees. So while men are following their lusts, they have checks of conscience, which are a foretaste of hell. Better to lack the honey, than have this sting. But violence for heaven is spiced with such joy, that it is not labor—but pleasure!

6. This violence and activity of spirit in piety, puts a luster upon a Christian. The more excellent anything is, the more active it is. The *sun* is a glorious creature, as a giant "it runs its race," Psalm xix. 5. *Fire*, the noblest element, sparkles vigorously. The *angels* are described with wings, Isaiah vi. 2. which is an emblem of their swift obedience. The more violent we are in piety, the more angelic we are!

7. How violent Christ was about our salvation! He was in agony; he "continued all night in prayer," Luke vi. 2. He wept, he fasted, he died a violent death; he rose violently out of the grave. Was Christ so violent for our salvation—and does it not befit us to be violent, who are so intimately concerned in it? Christ's violence was not only *substitutionary*—but *exemplary*. It was not only to appease God—but to teach us. Christ was violent in dying—to teach us to be violent in living and believing.

8. This holy violence brings rest. Motion tends to rest, Heb. iv. 9. "There remains a rest to the people of God." Indeed, there is a motion which does not tend to rest; those who are violent in a way of sin shall never have rest, Rev. iv. 8. "They have no rest, day and night." Such as are graceless, shall be restless. But the violence a Christian takes—leads to rest. As the weary traveler sits down at night and rests himself, Psalm cxvi. 7. "Return to your rest, O my soul." Holy violence is like the flying of Noah's dove to the ark, where it found rest.

9. If we use what violence we are able—God will help us. "It is God who works in you to will and to act according to his good purpose." Philippians 2:13. The Spirit helps us in prayer and so proportionately in all other duties of piety. "The Spirit helps us in our weakness." Romans 8:26. The promises *encourage*, and the Spirit *enables*. In all earthly races a man runs in his own strength; but in the race to Heaven we have the Spirit of God helping us; he not only gives us the crown, when we have finished running—but he gives us legs to run; he gives us quickening and assisting grace! The Spirit of God helping us makes our work easy. If another helps us to carry a burden, it is less difficult. If the magnet draws the iron—it is not hard for the iron to move. If the Spirit of God, as a divine magnet—draws and moves the heart in obedience, then the work goes on with more facility. "He gives strength to the weary and increases the power of the weak. Even youths grow tired and weary, and young men stumble and fall; but those who hope in the Lord will renew their strength. They will soar on wings like eagles; they will run and not grow weary, they will walk and not be faint." Isaiah 40:29-31

10. This blessed violence in piety, would be preventive of much sin. While men are *idle* in the vineyard, they are a prey to every temptation. Satan sows most of his *seed of temptation* in hearts which lie fallow. When he sees people unemployed, he will find work for them to do; he will stir them up to one sin or other. "While everyone was sleeping, his enemy came and sowed weeds among the wheat." Matthew 13:25. When Satan finds men in a drowsy condition, their sleeping time is his tempting time! But by holy violence, we prevent the Devil's design; we are so busy with salvation that we have no leisure to listen to temptation. Jerome advised his friend to be always well employed, that when Satan came with a temptation he might find him working in the vineyard. When the bird is flying, it is safe; when it sits still on the bough, it is in danger of being shot! When a Christian sits still and is inactive, then the Devil shoots him with his "fiery darts." "Watch and pray so that you will not fall into temptation!" Matthew 26:41.

11. Consider the folly of such as are violent for the world—but not for the glorious kingdom of heaven! Alas, how insipid are all these things that we lay out our sweat for and our violence upon! They will not make us happy. King Solomon distilled the quintessence out of all earthly things, and said, "behold, all is vanity," Eccles. ii. 8.

1. These earthly things that we toil so hard for, are **uncertain**, 1 Tim. vi. 17. It is uncertain whether we shall get them. All that are suitors to a virgin do not succeed. All that come to a lottery have not won a prize.

2. These earthly things that we toil so hard for, are **unsatisfactory**. Could men heap up silver as dust; had they as much as the Devil promised Christ, "All the kingdoms of

the world, and the glory of them;" yet they can no more fill the heart, than a drop of water can fill a cistern. Eccles. v. 16. "What profit has he that has labored for the wind?"

3.These earthly things that we toil so hard for, are **transient**; death feeds at the root. All worldly possessions are like a castle of snow in the sun; or like a posy of flowers, which withers while we are smelling them. Oh, folly is it to put forth all one's violence for the world, which is but "for a season," and not for Christ and grace. As if a condemned man being earnest to get his dinner—but not concerned with getting his pardon.

12. The next motive is in the text—this violence is for a kingdom! The kingdom of Heaven suffers violence. And what will we be violent for, if not for a kingdom? Men will wade to a kingdom through blood: this is a kingdom worth striving for. Cyprus is an island so exceedingly fertile and pleasant, that it was anciently called *Macaria*, which signifies *blessed*. This title of blessed may more fitly be given to the heavenly kingdom. If the mountains were gold; if every sand of the sea were a diamond; if the whole globe were a shining crysolite; it would all still be infinitely beneath the glory of this kingdom.

1. The BLESSINGS of the heavenly kingdom are great.

1. There shall be freedom from sin. Here on earth, sin keeps house with us; it is as natural to us to sin as to breathe. The soul that is most refined, and cleansed by grace, is not without some dregs of corruption. Paul cried out of a "body of sin." He who is inoculated into Christ still has a taste and relish of the wild olive tree. But when we ascend to the heavenly kingdom, this mantle of sin shall drop off. That kingdom is so pure, that it will not mix with any corruption. A sinful thought shall not creep in there. There is beauty which is not stained with lust, and honor which is not swelled with pride. "Nothing impure will ever enter it, nor will anyone who does what is shameful or deceitful, but only those whose names are written in the Lamb's book of life." Revelation 21:27

2. In that blessed kingdom there shall be freedom from the assaults of the red dragon. Tis sad to have Satan daily soliciting us by his temptations, and laboring to trick us into sin. Temptation is the Devil's powder plot to blow up the fort-royal of our grace; but this is the blessed freedom of the heavenly kingdom, it is not capable of temptation. The old serpent is cast out of Paradise.

3. In that blessed kingdom there shall be freedom from divisions. In this world God's own tribes go to war. Ephraim envies Judah, and Judah vexes Ephraim. **The soldier's spear pierced Christ's side—but the divisions of saints pierce his**

heart. Christ prayed that all his people might be one, as he and his Father are one, Jo. 17:21. But how do Christians by their discords and animosities go about with all their power to frustrate Christ's prayer! But in the kingdom of Heaven there is perfect love, which as it casts out fear, so it casts out strife. Those Christians that could not live quietly together here, in that kingdom shall be united. There Calvin and Luther are agreed. In that celestial kingdom there shall be no vilifying or slandering one another, no raking into those sores which Christ died to heal. Christians who could not pray together, shall sing together in that glorious choir: there shall not be one jarring string in the saints" music.

4. In that heavenly kingdom there shall be freedom from all afflictions. Our lives now are interlined with troubles. "My life is consumed by anguish and my years by groaning; my strength fails because of my affliction, and my bones grow weak." Psalm 31:10. There are many things to occasion disquiet; sometimes *poverty* afflicts; sometimes *sickness* tortures; sometimes *unkindness* of friends breaks the heart. Our lives, like the seas, are full of tempests. But in the kingdom of Heaven, there is nothing to give grief. There, all is serene and calm; nothing within to trouble, or without to molest.

2. The royalties and EXCELLENCIES of that heavenly kingdom are great. We may say of Heaven, as it was said of Laish, Judges xviii. 9,10. "We have seen the land, and, behold, it is very good; a place where there is no lack of anything"

2. The heavenly kingdom abounds with RICHES! Rev. xxi. 27. "The twelve gates were twelve pearls." Earthly kingdoms are glad to traffic abroad for gold and spices. In the kingdom of God, all rarities are to be had, all commodities are of its own growth, therefore figured by the tree of life bearing several sorts of fruit, Rev. xxii. 2. How rich is that place where the blessed Deity shines forth in its immense glory infinitely beyond the comprehension of angels!

2. The delights of the heavenly kingdom are UNMIXED. The comforts here below are checkered. Honor may be stained with disgrace; joy interwoven with sorrow. Our stars are mixed with clouds; but the delicacies of heaven are pure as well as pleasant. There is honey that has not one drop of gall. The crystal spring of joy has no *settlings of sorrow* at the bottom. The rose in that paradise is without prickles; the sun in that horizon is without eclipse.

3. This kingdom above is DURABLE. Suppose earthly kingdoms to be more glorious than they are, their foundations of gold, their walls of pearl, their windows of sapphire—yet they are still corruptible, Hos. i. 1. "I will cause the kingdom to cease." Troy and Athens now lie buried in their own ruins. But the kingdom of glory, as it is made without hands—so it is without end. It is "the everlasting kingdom," 2 Pet. i. 11.

Now, methinks, that if we ever will use violence, it should be for this kingdom; this kingdom will make amends for all our labor and pains. Caesar, marching towards Rome, and hearing that all the people were fled from it, said, they will not fight for this city, what city will they fight for? So if we will not put forth violence for this Kingdom of Heaven, what will we be violent for? I say to all, as the children of Dan in another sense, Judges xviii. 9. "We have seen the land, and behold, it is very good; and are you still? Be not slothful to go, and to enter to possess the land."

13. The more violence we have used for Heaven—the sweeter Heaven will be when we come there. As when a man has been grafting trees, or setting flowers in his garden, it is pleasant to review and look over his labors: so in Heaven, when we shall remember our former zeal and activity for the kingdom, it will enhance Heaven, and add to the joy of it. For a Christian to think, "Such a day I spent in examining my heart; such a day I was weeping for sin; when others were at their sport, I was at my prayers. And now, have I lost anything by this violence? My tears are wiped away, and the wine of paradise cheers my heart. I now enjoy him whom my soul loves! I now have the crown and white robes I so longed for!" O how pleasant will it be to think—this is the Heaven my Savior bled for, and I sweat for!

14. The more violence we put forth in piety, the greater measure of glory we shall have. That there are degrees in glory in Heaven seems to me beyond dispute.

1. There are degrees of torment in Hell; therefore, by the rule of contraries, there are degrees of glory in Heaven.

2. The Scripture speaks of a prophet's reward, Matt. x. 41. which is a degree above others.

3. The saints are said to shine as the stars, Dan. xii. One star differs from another in glory. So that there are gradations of happiness; and of this judgment is Calvin; as also many of the ancient fathers.

Consider then seriously, the more violent we are for Heaven, and the more work we do for God, the greater will be our reward. The hotter our zeal, the brighter our crown. Could we hear the blessed souls departed speaking to us from Heaven, surely they would say, "Were we to leave heaven awhile and to dwell on the earth again, we would do God a thousand times more service than we have ever done! We would pray with more life, act with more zeal; for now we see that the more we have labored, the more astonishing is our joy and the more flourishing our crown!"

15. Upon our violence for the kingdom God has promised mercy. Matt. vii. 7. "Ask and it shall be given you; seek, and you shall find; knock, and it shall be opened unto you."

1. **ASK.** Ask with importunity. A faint asking begs a denial. King Ahasuerus stood with his golden scepter and said to queen Esther, "Ask, and it shall be given, to the half of the kingdom!" But God says more, "Ask and he will give you the whole kingdom!" Luke xii. 32. It is observable, that the door of the tabernacle was not of brass—but had a thin covering, a veil, that they might easily enter into it. Just so, the door of Heaven is made easy through Christ's blood, that our prayers put up in fervency may enter. Upon our asking, God has promised to give his spirit, Luke xi.13. And if he gives his Spirit, he will give his kingdom; the Spirit first anoints, 1 John ii. 27, and after his anointing oil comes the crown.

2. **"SEEK**, and you shall find." But, is it not said, "Many will seek to enter in, and shall not be able?" Luke xiii. 24. I answer, that that is because they seek in a wrong manner.

1. They did seek **ignorantly**, setting up an altar to the unknown god. It is hard seeking pearls in the dark. Ignorant people seek Heaven by their good meanings; they seek in the dark, and no wonder they miss salvation.

2. They did seek **proudly**. They sought Heaven by their own merits; whereas we are to seek the kingdom in Christ's strength, and in his Name.

3. They did seek **lazily**; as the spouse sought Christ on her bed and found him not, Cant. iii. 1. So many seek Christ in a supine manner; they *seek*—but they do not *strive*.

4. They did seek **hypocritically**. They would have Heaven and their lusts too. But let not such seekers ever think to find happiness; let them not think they can lie in Delilah's lap--and go to Abraham's bosom when they die.

5. They did seek **inconstantly**. Because mercy did not come immediately, they gave over seeking.

But if we seek the kingdom of Heaven cordially, God has pawned his truth in a promise, and we shall find, Jer xxix. 13. "Then shall you find me, when you shall search for Me with all your heart."

3. **"KNOCK**, and it shall be opened." Knocking implies violence. But we must do as Peter, Acts xii. 16. "He continued knocking," We must continue knocking by prayer,

and Heaven-gate shall be opened. How may this be as oil to the wheels? how may it encourage holy violence when we have so gracious a promise of mercy upon our earnest seeking of it.

16. This holy violence will not hinder men in their secular employments. Violence for the kingdom, and, diligence in a calling, are not inconsistent. Christians, you may work for Heaven—yet work in a trade. God has given you a *body* and a *soul,*and he has allotted you time to provide for both. He has given you a *body*, therefore be diligent in your calling; he has given you a soul, therefore be violent for Heaven. These two may well stand together— providing for a family and praying in a family. He who does not exercise himself in some honest employment, is guilty of the breach of that commandment, six days shall you labor. God never sealed warrants for idleness. The sluggard shall be indicted at the day of judgment for letting his field be over-run with thorns. They are hypocrites who talk of living by faith but refuse to live in a calling. Only remember that the pains you take in piety must exceed the other, Matt. vii. 33, "Seek *first* the kingdom of God." First, in order of time, *before* all things; and first in order of affection, *above* all things. Your soul is the nobler part, therefore that must be chiefly looked after. In your calling show diligence; in piety, show violence.

But some may say, we are so encumbered in the world that all time for piety is swallowed up; we cannot get a break from our calling to read or pray?

If your trade is such that you cannot allow yourselves time for your souls—then your trade is unlawful. There are two things that make a trade unlawful.

1. When people deal in such commodities as they know cannot be used without sin, such as selling on the black market or selling idolatrous pictures and crucifixes.

2. When their trade so involves them in worldly business, that they cannot mind eternity, or make out one sally to the throne of grace. They are so much in the shop—that they cannot be in the closet. If there be such a trade to be found, doubtless it is unlawful. But let not men lay this problem upon their trade—but upon themselves; their *trade* would give them leave to serve God—but their *covetousness* will not give them leave. O how many put a fallacy upon their own souls—and cheat themselves into hell.

17. There is but a short space of time granted us, therefore, work the harder for Heaven before it be too late. Indeed we are apt to dream of a long life, as if we were not sojourners but natives, and would reside here always. The blossom of childhood hopes to come to the budding of youth; and the bud of youth hopes to come to the flower of mature age; and the flower of mature age hopes to come come to old age;

and old age hopes to renew its strength as the eagle. But if we measure life by a pair of scripture-compasses, it is very short: it is compared to a "flying shadow," Job viii. 17, to a "handbreadth," Psalm xxxix. 5. as if there were but a span between the cradle and the grave. Is the time of life so short, and maybe shorter than we are aware? What need is there to zealously improve it before it has slipped away? If time runs, let us 'so run," 1 Cor. ix. 24. He who has a great business in hand, and the time allotted for doing it is but short, should not lose any of that time. A traveler that has many miles to ride, and the night is ready to approach, had need spur on the harder, that the night does not overtake him. Just so, we have a long journey, the night of death is drawing on, how we should use spurs to our sluggish hearts, that we may go on more swiftly!

18. A man's personal day of grace may be short. There is a time in which the scepter of grace is held forth, 2 Cor vi. 2. "Now is the accepted time." The Lord has prefixed a time wherein the means of grace shall or shall not work. If a person does not come in, by such a time, God may say, "Never shall fruit grow on you anymore." A sign that this day of grace, is past is when conscience no longer speaks and God's Spirit has done striving. Whether this day may be longer or shorter, we cannot tell; but because it may transpire so soon, it is wisdom to take the present opportunity, and use all violence for Heaven. The day of hastens away. No man can (like Joshua) bid this 'sun stand still;" and if this critical day be once past, it cannot be recalled. **The day of grace being lost—the next is a day of wrath!**

Jerusalem had a day—but she lost it, Luke xix. 44. "If you had known, even you, at least in this your day, the things which belong unto your peace—but now they are hid from your eyes." After the expiration of the day of grace, no means or mercies shall prove effectual. Now, "they are hid from your eyes." Which is like the ringing of a doleful knell over a dying person; therefore, put forth all violence for Heaven and do it in this "your day," before it be too late and the decree be gone forth.

19. If you neglect the offering of violence, now—there will be no help for you after death. When men shall open their eyes in another world and see into what a damned condition they have sinned themselves, O now what would they not do— what violence would they now use—if there were a possibility they might be saved!

When once the door of mercy is shut, if God would make new terms far harder than before, they would readily agree to them. If God should say to the sinner after death, would you be content to return to the earth, and live there under the harrow of persecution a thousand years for my sake? "Yes, Lord, I will subscribe to this, and endure the world's fury—that I may have but your favor at last!"

"But will you be content to serve an apprenticeship in Hell a thousand years, where you shall feel the worm gnawing and the fire burning?" "Yes, Lord, even in Hell I submit to you; so that after a thousand years I may have a release and that "bitter cup" may pass away from me!"

"But, will you, for every lie you have told endure the rack? will you for every oath that you have sworn, fill a bottle of tears? will you for every sin you have committed lie ten thousand years in sackcloth and ashes?" "Yes, Lord, all this and more if you require, I will subscribe to; I am content now to use any violence if I may but at last be admitted into your kingdom!"

"No!" God will say, "there shall be no such condition proposed to you, no possibility of favor—but you shall lie forever among the damned; and who is able to dwell with everlasting burnings?"

Oh, therefore be wise in time, now while God's terms are more easy, embrace Christ and Heaven, for after death there will be nothing to be done for your souls.
The *sinner* and the *fiery furnace* shall never be parted!

20. How without all defense will you be left, if you neglect this violence for Heaven! Methinks I hear God thus expostulating the case with sinners thus at the last day: "Why did you not take pains for Heaven? Has there not been a prophet among you? Did not my ministers lift up their voice like a trumpet? did not they warn you? did not they persuade you to use this violence, telling you that your salvation depended upon it? But the most melting rhetoric of the gospel would not move you. Did I not give you time to look after your souls? (Rev. ii. 21. "I gave her space to repent.") Did not you promise in your vow in baptism, that you would take Heaven by force? 'fighting under my banner against world, flesh, and Devil?' Why then did you not use violence for the kingdom? It must be either sloth or obstinacy. You could be violent for other things, for the world, for your lusts—but not for the kingdom of Heaven! What can you say for yourselves, as to why the sentence of damnation should not pass?"

O how will men be confounded, and left speechless at such a time, and God's justice shall be cleared in their condemnation! Psalm li. 4. "That you might be clear when you judge." **Though the sinner shall drink a sea of wrath—yet he shall not drink one drop of injustice!**

21. What a vexation it will be at the last to lose the kingdom of glory for lack of a little violence. When one shall think with himself, "I did something in piety—but I was not violent enough. I prayed—but I should have brought fire to the sacrifice. I heard the word—but I should have received the truth in love. I humbled myself with fasting—but I should with humiliation have joined reformation. I gave Christ's poor good words; I did bid them be warmed—but I should have clothed and fed them. For lack of a little more violence I have lost the kingdom!"

The prophet bade the king of Israel smite upon the ground, 2 Kings 13:18,19. And he "He struck it three times and stopped. The man of God was angry with him and said, "You should have struck the ground five or six times; then you would have defeated Aram and completely destroyed it." So a man does something in piety, "he strikes three times and then stops; whereas had he but put forth a little more violence for Heaven he would have been saved. What a mischief is this, but to half do one's work, and by shooting short—to lose the kingdom! O how will this cut a man to the heart when he is in hell to think, "had I but gone a little further it had been better with me than it is now; I had not been tormented thus in the flame!"

22. The examples of the saints of old, who have taken heaven by force. David broke his sleep for meditation, Psalm 119:148. His violence for heaven was boiled up to zeal, Psalm 119:39. "My zeal has consumed me!" And Paul *"pressed on* to take hold of that for which Christ Jesus took hold of me." The Greek Word signifies to stretch out the neck: it is a metaphor taken from racers, who strain every limb, and reach forward to lay hold upon the prize. We read of Anna, a prophetess, Luke ii. 37. "She departed not from the temple—but served God with fastings and prayers night and day." How industrious was Calvin in the Lord's vineyard. When his friends persuaded him for his health's sake, to remit a little of his labors, says he, "Would you have the Lord find me idle when he comes?" Luther spent three hours a day in prayer. It is said of holy Bradford, that preaching, reading, and prayer were his whole life. I rejoice (said Jewel) that my body is exhausted in the labors of my holy calling. How violent were the blessed martyrs! They wore their fetters as ornaments; they snatched up torments as crowns, and embraced the flames as cheerfully as Elijah did the fiery chariot which came to fetch him to Heaven. "Let racks, fires, pulleys, and all manner of torments come—just so I may win Christ!" said Ignatius. These pious souls resisted unto blood. How should these provoke our zeal! Write after these fair copies.

23. If the saints with all their violence have much ado to get to heaven, how shall they come there, who use no violence? 1 Peter ix. 18. "If the righteous scarcely are saved, where shall the ungodly and the sinner appear?" If they who strive as in an agony can hardly get in at the strait gate—what shall become of those who never strive at all? If Paul did "keep under his body," by prayer, watching, and fasting, 1 Cor. ix. 27, how shall they be saved, who wholly let loose the reins to the flesh, and bathe themselves in the luscious streams of carnal pleasure?

24. This sweating for Heaven is not to endure long. 1 Peter v. 10. "After you have suffered a while." So after you have offered violence a while, there shall be an end put to it. Your labor shall expire with your life! It is but a little while—and you will be done weeping, wrestling, and praying! It is but a little while—and the race will be over, and you shall receive "the end of your faith, the salvation of your souls," 1 Pet. i.9. It is but a little while—and and you shall be done your weary marches, you shall put off your armor and put on white robes! How should this excite a spirit of holy violence! It is but a few months or days—and you shall reap the sweet fruit of your obedience! The winter will be past, and the spring flowers of joy shall appear. Doctor Taylor comforted himself when he was going to the stake, "I have but two stiles to go over—and I shall be at my Father's house!" Christians, you have but a little way to go, a little more violence, a few more tears to shed, a few more Sabbaths to keep, and then your hopes shall be crowned with the beatifical sight of God! When the vapor is blown away—then we may see the sun clearly. Just so, when this short vapor of life is blown away—then we shall behold Christ, the Sun of Righteousness, in all his glory! 1 John iii. 2. "We shall see him as he is!"

25. If you are not violent for Heaven, you walk contrary to your own prayers. You pray that God's will may be done by you on earth, "as it is done in Heaven." Now how is God's will done in Heaven? Are not the angels swift in doing the will of God, like the stars above, which are moved many millions of miles in an hour. The seraphim are described with wings—to show how swift and winged they are in their obedience, Isaiah vi. 2. Now if you are not violent in your spiritual motion, you live in a contradiction to your own prayers. You are far from being as *angels*; you creep as *snails* in the way to Heaven.

26. This holy and blessed violence would make Christians willing to die. What makes men so loathe to die? Why so? Because their conscience accuses them that they have taken little or no pains for Heaven! They have been sleeping, when they should have been working, and now death looks ghastly! They are afraid death will carry them as prisoners to hell!

Whereas the Christian who has been active in piety, and has spent his time in the service of God, can look death in the face with comfort. He who has been violent for Heaven in this life need not fear a violent death. Death shall do him no hurt; it shall not be a destruction—but a deliverance; it shall purge out sin and perfect glory! What made Paul say, "I desire to depart and be with Christ, which is better by far!" Phil. i. 23. Surely the reason was, that he had been a man of violence; he did spend himself for Christ, and labored more than all the other Apostles. 1 Cor. xv. 10. And now he knew there was a crown laid up for him. Augustus desired that he might have a quiet, easy death. If anything will make our pillow easy at death, and make us go out of the world quietly—it will be this holy violence that we have put forth in the business of piety.

27. If for all that has been said you will either sit still, or keep your sweat for something other than Heaven, know, that there is a time coming shortly when you will wish you had used this violence. When sickness seizes you, and your disease begins to grow violent, and you think God's sergeant is at the door—what wishes will you make, "O that I had been more violent for heaven! O that I had been praying—when I was dancing and making merry! O that I had had a bible in my hand—when I had a hand of cards! How happy then might I have been! But alas, my case is miserable! What shall I do! I am so sick—that I cannot *live;* and so sinful— that I dare not *die?* O that God would respite me a little longer, that he would put a few more years in my lease, that a little space might be granted me to recover my lost hours!"

As one said on her death-bed, "Call time again!" But time will not be called back again. At the hour of death, sinners will awaken out of their lethargy—and fall into a frenzy of horror and despair!

Shall not all these arguments prevail with men to be violent for the kingdom? What a hardened rock, is a sinner's heart! We read that at Christ's passion, the rocks rent, Matt. xxvii. 51. But nothing will move a sinner. The rocks will sooner rend—than his heart. If all that I have said will not prevail, it is a sign that ruin is at hand! 1 Sam ii. 25. "They hearkened not unto the voice of their Father, because the Lord would slay them!"

Yet this caution I must necessarily insert—Though we shall not obtain the kingdom *without* violence—yet it shall not be obtained *for* our violence. When we have done all, look up to Christ and free grace! Though we are saved in the use of means—yet it is by grace too, Ephes. ii. 5. "By grace you are saved." Heaven is a *gift.* Luke xii. 32. "It is your Father's good pleasure to *give* you the kingdom." One may say, "I have used violence for it, I have wrought for the kingdom—but it is a gift which free grace bestows!" We must look up to Christ for acceptance. It is not our sweat—but his blood which saves. Our laboring qualifies us for Heaven—but Christ's dying purchased Heaven!

Alas, what is all that we have done—compared with glory? What is the shedding of a tear—compared to a crown? Therefore we must renounce all in terms of our justification, and let Christ and free grace carry away the glory of our salvation. God must help us in our working, Phil ii. 11. "It is God who works in you both to will and to do." How then can we merit by our working, when it is God who helps us in our working?

Hindrances, Directions, and Conclusions

I shall, in the next place, lay down some rules or directions on how to get this blessed violence.

1. Take heed of those things which will HINDER this violence for Heaven.

1. If you would be violent for Heaven—take heed of UNBELIEF. Unbelief is a great impediment, for it is discouraging. When a Christian is working for Heaven, unbelief whispers thus, "To what purpose are all these pains? I might just as well sit still. I may pray, and not be heard; I may work, and have no reward; I may come near heaven—yet miss it!" Jer viii.12. "And they said, there is no hope." Unbelief destroys hope; and if you cut this sinew of piety, all violence for Heaven ceases. Unbelief raises a cloud of despondency in the heart. "Alas, you will never be able to go through the work of piety. There are so many precepts to obey; so many temptations to resist; so many afflictions to bear—that you will fall under the heavy burden; you will tire in your march to Heaven!"

Unbelief raises jealous thoughts of God, it represents him as an austere master, and that if we fail in so little a punctilio, he will take the extremity of the law upon us. This discourages the soul in the use of means. Unbelief does as Sanballat and Tobiah and to the Jews, Nehem. vi. 9. "They all made us afraid, saying, Their hands shall be weakened from the work." O take heed of unbelief; it destroys this holy violence. We read of Jeroboam's arm being withered, 1 Kings xiii. 4. **Unbelief withers the arm of the soul, that it cannot stretch itself forth to any spiritual action!** Unbelief does the Devil the greatest kindness; it makes way for his temptations to enter, which do so enchant and bewitch us, that we cannot work. Beware of this sin—believe the promises! God "is good to the soul that seeks him," Lam. iii. 25. Do but seek him with importunity, and he will open both his heart and Heaven to you!

2. If you would be violent for Heaven—take heed of puzzling your thoughts about ELECTION. A Christian may think thus, "Why should I take pains? Perhaps I am not elected, and then all my violence is to no purpose!" Thus many are taken off from the use of means and the business of piety comes to a stand-still. Whereas the truth is—that no man can justly say he is not elected. It is true, some of God's children have said so in temptation; but, as Peter did not know what he was saying at Christ's transfiguration; so these in temptation. But no man can say on just grounds, that he is not elected, unless he can prove that he has sinned the unpardonable sin against the Holy Spirit. For anyone to assert non-election is a sin; for that which keeps him in sin must needs be sinful. But this opinion keeps him in sin; it discourages him from the use of means and cuts the sinews of all endeavors! Do not therefore perplex your thoughts about election. The book of election is sealed, and no angel can unclasp it. The rule Christians are to go by is, God's *revealed* will, not his *secret* will. God's revealed will is, that we should pray and repent; by this we make our calling sure; and by making our calling sure, we make our election sure. If I see the beds of spices grow and flourish, I know the sun has been there. Just so, if I find the fruits of obedience in my heart, I may conclude God's electing love has shined upon me! 2 Thes. ii. 13. "God has from the beginning chosen you to salvation through sanctification."

3. If you would be violent for Heaven—take heed of too much violence after the WORLD. The world cools holy affections. The earth puts out the fire. The world's silver trumpet sounds a retreat—and calls men away from their pursuit after Heaven. The world hindered the young man from following Christ, "he went away sorrowful!" Whereupon, says our Savior, "How hard it is for the rich to enter the kingdom of God!" Luke 18:24. Demas' piety was buried in the earth, 2 Tim iv. 10. "Demas has forsaken me—having loved this present world." Jonathan pursued the victory until he came to the honeycomb, and then he stood still, 1 Sam. xiv. 27. Many are violent for the kingdom of God, until gain or preferment offers itself; when they meet with this honey, then they stand still. The world blinds men's eyes that they do not see the narrow way to heaven! It fetters their feet that they do not run in the way of God's commandments. Mithridates, king of Pontus, being beaten by the Romans, and fearing he would not escape them—caused a great deal of silver and gold to be scattered in the ways, which while the Roman soldiers were busy gathering, he got away from them. The like stratagem Satan uses; knowing what tempting things riches are, he throws them as baits, in men's way, that while they are eagerly gathering these, he may hinder them in their pursuit of eternal happiness.

I have observed some who did once, Jehu like, drive on furiously in the cause of piety; when the world has come in upon them their chariot-wheels have been pulled off, and they have "driven on heavily!" It would hinder a man to climb up a steep rock, with heavy weights tied to his legs. Men's golden weights hinder them in climbing up this steep rock which leads to salvation. The *world's music* charms men asleep, and when they are asleep, they are not fit to work. A thing cannot be carried violently to two extremes at once. The ship cannot go full sail to the east and west at the same time. Just so, a man cannot be violent for Heaven and earth at once: he may have Christ and the world—but cannot love Christ and the world, 1 John ii. 15. He who is all on fire for the world, will be all ice for Heaven. Take heed of engaging your affections too far in these earthly things. Use the world as your servant—but do not follow it as your master.

4. If you would be violent for Heaven, take heed of indulging any LUST. Indulging in sin, will spoil all effort for Heaven. Sin enfeebles; it is like the cutting of Samson's hair—then the strength departs. Sin is the soul's sickness. Sickness takes a man off his legs and so dispirits him that he is unfit for any violent exercise. A sick man cannot run a race. Sin lived in, takes a man quite off from duty, or makes him dead in it. The more lively the heart is in sin, the more dead it is in prayer. How can he be earnest with God for mercy, whose heart accuses him of secret sin? Guilt breeds fear, and that which strengthens fear, weakens violence. Adam, having sinned—was afraid and hid himself, Gen. iii. 10. When Adam had lost his innocence—he lost his violence.

Therefore lay the axe to the root! Let sin be hewn down! Do not only abstain from sin in the act--but let the love of sin be mortified, and let every sin be put to the sword! Many will leave all their sins but one. They save one sin --and lose one soul! One sin is a fetter! A man may lose the race as well by having one fetter on his leg—just as if

he had many. I have read of a great monarch, who, fleeing from his enemy, threw away the crown of gold on his head--that he might run the faster. So, that sin which you wore as a crown of gold--throw it away that you may run the faster to the heavenly kingdom!

5. If you would be violent for Heaven, take heed of DESPONDENCY of spirit. Be serious, but cheerful. He whose spirit is pressed down with sadness, is unfit to go about his work. An uncheerful heart is unfit to pray, or praise God. When the strings of a lute are *wet*, it will not put forth any sweet harmony. Such as go drooping under fears and discouragements cannot be violent in piety. When a soldier faints in the field, he soon lets his sword fall. David chides himself out of his melancholy, Psalm. xliii. 5. "Why are you cast down, O my soul? Why are you disquieted within me? Hope in God!" A sad heart makes dull action. We use the drum and trumpet in battle, that the noise of the trumpet may excite and quicken the soldiers spirits, and make them fight more vigorously. Cheerfulness is like music in battle; it excites a Christian's spirits and makes him vigorous and lively in duty. What is done with cheerfulness is done with delight—and the soul flies most swiftly to Heaven upon the wings of delight!

6. If you would be violent for Heaven, take heed of a slothful, LAZY disposition. A slothful Christian is like a fearful soldier, who has a good desire for the plunder—but is loathe to storm the castle. A slothful person would gladly have Heaven—but is loathe to take it by storm. Sloth is the soul's sleep. Many instead of working out salvation, sleep away salvation. Such as will not labor, must be put at last to beg. They must beg, as Dives in hell--for one drop of water. An idle man (says Solomon) "puts his hand in his bosom," Proverbs xix. 24. He should have his hand to the *plough*, and he puts it in *bosom*. God never made Heaven a hive for drones. Sloth is a disease apt to grow upon men—shake it off! A sluggish ship is a prey to the pirate. A sluggish soul is a prey to Satan. When the crocodile sleeps with his mouth open—the rat gets into his belly and eats his entrails. Just so, while men are asleep in sloth—the Devil enters and devours them!

7. If you would be violent for Heaven, take heed of consulting with flesh and blood. As good consult with the Devil as the flesh. The flesh is a bosom traitor. An enemy within the walls is the worst enemy. The flesh cries out, there is a "lion in the way!" The flesh will bid you, 'spare yourself!" as Peter did Christ. "O, do not be so violent for Heaven, spare yourself." The flesh says as Judas, "Why all this waste?" "Why all this praying and wrestling? Why do you waste your strength? Why all this waste?" The flesh cries out for ease; it is loathe to put its neck under Christ's yoke. The flesh is for pleasure; it would rather be playing gaimes—than running the heavenly race. There is a description of fleshly pleasures, "You lie on beds inlaid with ivory and lounge on your couches. You dine on choice lambs and fattened calves. You strum away on your harps like David and improvise on musical instruments. You drink wine by the bowlful and use the finest lotions." Amos 6:4-6. These are the delights of the flesh.

There was one who tried to please all of his five senses at once. He had a room richly decorated with beautiful pictures; he had the most delectable music; he had all the choice aromatics and perfumes; he had all the sumptuous candies of the confectioner; he was lodged in bed with a beautiful paramour. Thus he indulged the flesh, and swore that he would spend all his estate to live one week like like this—though he were sure to be damned in hell the next day. "There was a rich man who was dressed in purple and fine linen and lived in luxury every day. In hell, where he was in torment, he looked up and saw Abraham far away, with Lazarus by his side. So he called to him, 'Father Abraham, have pity on me and send Lazarus to dip the tip of his finger in water and cool my tongue, because I am in agony in this fire!'" Luke 16:19, 23-24

O take heed of holding intelligence with the flesh! The flesh is a bad Counselor. Paul would "not confer with flesh and blood," Gal. i. 16. The flesh is a sworn enemy to this holy violence. "For if you live after the flesh—you shall die! But if you through the Spirit do mortify the deeds of the body—you shall live." Romans 8:13

8. If you would be violent for Heaven, take heed of listening to the voice of such carnal friends, as they will call you away from this blessed violence. Fire when in snow, will soon lose its heat and by degrees go out. Among bad company you will soon lose your heat for piety. The company of the wicked will sooner cool you—than your company will heat them. Vinegar will sooner sour the wine—than the wine will sweeten the vinegar. How often do carnal friends do the same to our souls—as infected people do to our bodies by conveying the plague. The wicked are still dissuading us from this violence; they will say that it is needless preciseness and singularity; just as Christ's friends laid hold on him when he was going to preach, Mark iii. 21. "They went to take charge of him, for they said—He is out of his mind." Such as are unacquainted with the spirituality and sweetness of piety, judge all

Christian zeal to be madness; and therefore will lay hold upon us to hinder us in this sacred violence.

When we are earnest suitors to piety, our carnal friends will raise some bad report of it, and so endeavor to break the match. Galeacius, marquis of Vico, being resolved for Heaven—what a block in his way did he find his carnal relations! and what ado he had to endure to break through that impediment!

Take heed of the snare in your family! It is one of the Devil's great subtleties, to hinder us from piety by our nearest relations, and to shoot us with our own rib! He tempted Adam by his wife, Gen. iii. 6. Who would have suspected the Devil there? He handed over a temptation to Job by his wife, Job ii. 9. "Do you still retain your integrity?" "What, notwithstanding all these disasters that have befallen you, do you still pray and serve God? Throw off his yoke; curse God and die!" Thus would the Devil have cooled Job's love for God; but the shield of his faith quenched this fiery dart.

Spira's friends stood in his way to Heaven. For consulting with them about Luther's doctrine, they persuaded him to recant, and so openly abjuring his former faith, he felt a hell in his conscience. Take heed of such tempters; resolve to hold on your violence for Heaven, though your carnal friends dissuade you. It is better to go to Heaven with their hatred—than to Hell with their love. It was a saying of Hierom, "If my parents should persuade me to deny Christ; if my wife should go to charm me with her embraces, I would forsake all and fly to Christ!" **It is better to go to Heaven with their hatred—than to Hell with their love! If our dearest friends and family lie in our way to Heaven—we must either leap over them, or tread upon them!** "A man's enemies will be the members of his own household. Anyone who loves his father or mother more than me is not worthy of me; anyone who loves his son or daughter more than me is not worthy of me; and anyone who does not take his cross and follow me is not worthy of me." Matthew 10:36-38

9. If you would be violent for Heaven, take heed of setting up your abode in the lowest pitch of grace. He who has the least grace, may have *motion*, but not *violence*. It is a pitiful thing to be contented with just so much grace as will keep life and soul together. A sick man may have life—but is not lively. Grace may live in the heart—but is sickly, and does not flourish into lively acts. Weak grace will not withstand strong temptations, or carry us through great sufferings; it will hardly follow Christ upon the water. Little grace will not do God much service. A tree which has but little sap—will not have much fruit. It may be said of some Christians, though they are not stillborn—yet they are stunted in grace. They are like a ship which comes with much difficulty, to the haven. Oh, labor to grow to further degrees of sanctity. The more grace, the more strength; and the more strength, the more violence. "But grow in the grace and knowledge of our Lord and Savior Jesus Christ. To him be glory both now and forever!" Amen. 2 Peter 3:18

10. If you would be violent for Heaven, take heed of the opinion that it is not so hard to get the kingdom; hence, less violence will serve. He who thinks he need not run a race so fast, will be apt to slacken his pace. This has undone many. Who will take pains for Heaven, who thinks that it may be had at a cheaper rate? But if it be so easy, what need was there for Christ to say, strive as in an agony. What did Paul need to beat down his body? Why does the text speak of taking the kingdom by force? Is not conversion called a "new birth" and "a new creation"? Is that easy? O take heed of imagining that that work easy—which is both above nature and against it. It is as great a wonder for a soul to be saved—as to see a mill-stone flying up to the moon!

If you would be violent for Heaven, use those MEANS which will promote this holy violence.

1. If you would be violent for Heaven—keep up daily PRAYER. Prayer is the bellows which blows up the affections. A Christian is most active, when his affections are most violent. Prayer keeps the trade of piety going. Prayer is to the soul, as the heart is to the body; the heart makes the body agile and lively; so does prayer for the soul. That the motion of a watch may be quicker, the spring must be wound up. Christian, wind up your heart every day by prayer. Prayer fetches in strength from Christ; and when his strength comes in, it sets the soul to work. Prayer leaves the heart in a holy frame—as the morning sun leaves a warmth in the room for the rest of the day. When Christians lay aside prayer, or leave off fervency in it—then by degrees they lose their holy violence.

2. If you would be violent for Heaven—get under godly PREACHING. The Word is "living and powerful," Heb. iv. 12. It puts life into a dead heart. It is both a sword to cut down sin, and a spur to quicken grace. The Word is a fire to thaw a frozen heart, Jer xxiii. 29. "Is not my Word fire?" As good almost be without preaching, as to be under such preaching as will not warm us. The Word not only *informs*—but *inflames*. Psalm 119:50, "Your Word has quickened me." Tis the lively dispensation of the oracles of Heaven, which must animate us, and make us lively in our duties.

3. If you would be violent for Heaven—get your hearts filled with love to piety. This is like the myrtle staff in the traveler's hand, (Pliny speaks of) which makes him fresh and lively in his travel, and keeps him from becoming weary. When a man has warmed himself by the fire, he is fittest for work. If you would be violent in working out salvation, warm yourselves by this fire of love. A man will only strive for that which he loves. Why are men so eager in their pursuit after gold—but because they love it? Love causes delight, and delight causes violence. What made Paul labor more than all the other apostles? "Christ's love compels us!" 2 Corinthians 5:14. Love is like oil to the wheels. Get love for piety and you will never be weary; you will count those the best hours which are spent with God. He who digs in a gold mine sweats—yet love for the gold makes his labor delightful.

4. If you would be violent for Heaven—be vigilant. The prophet stood upon his "watch tower," Hab. ii.1. Why are Christians so listless in their work—but because they are so careless in their watch. Did they but watch to see how their **enemy**watches, they would be violent to resist him! Did they but watch to see how fast their **time** runs, or rather flies, they would be violent to redeem it! Did they but watch to see how their **hearts** loiter in piety, they would spur on faster to Heaven. The reason there is so little violence in piety—is because there is so little vigilance. When Christians neglect their spiritual watch, and grow secure, then their motion to Heaven is retarded and Satan's motions to sin are renewed. **Our sleeping time is Satan's tempting time!**

5. If you would be violent for Heaven—bind your heart to God by sacred vows. A servant will be more diligent after he is bound to his master. Vow to the Lord that by his grace you will act more vigorously in the sphere of piety, Psalm. lvi. 12. "Your vows are upon me, O God." A vow binds the votary to duty. He then looks upon himself as under a special obligation—and that quickens endeavor. No question but a Christian may make such a vow, because the ground of it is morally good. He vows nothing but what he is bound to do, namely, to walk more closely with God. Only remember, that we do not vow in our own strength—but Christ's. We must confide in him as well for strength as for righteousness. Isaiah xlv. 24. "In the Lord have I righteousness and strength."

6. If you would be violent for Heaven—be sure you make going to Heaven your main business. Whatever a man looks on with indifference—he will never be violent for. But that which he makes his main business—he will be industrious about. A man looks upon his trade as the only thing to get a livelihood by—and he follows it closely. Just so, if we would but look upon piety as the main business wherein our salvation is concerned, we would be violent in it. Luke x. 42. "But one thing is needful." This is the one thing, to get Christ and Heaven—this is the end we came into the world for! If we could thus look upon the things of eternity as our business—the one thing—how earnest would we be in the pursuit of them!

7. If you would be violent for Heaven—have Heaven continually in your eye. This made Christ violent to death; he had an eye to the joy set before him, Heb. xii. 2. Set the crown ever before you, and that will provoke endeavor.

The mariner has his *hand* to the stern, and his *eye* to the star. While we are working, let us have an eye to that place where Christ is, the bright morning Star. How willingly does a man wades through deep water, when he sees dry land before him, and is sure to be crowned as soon as he comes to shore! Every time you cast your eyes up to Heaven, think, "Above that starry heaven, is the celestial Heaven which I am striving for!" Thus did Moses; the *eye of his faith* quickened the feet of his obedience, Heb. xi. 26. "He looked to the recompense of the reward." When Christians lose their prospect of Heaven, then they begin to slacken their pace in the way there.

8. If you would be violent for Heaven—keep company with such as are violent. When we need fire—we go to our neighbor's hearth and fetch fire. Often be among the godly, and so you shall fetch some heat and quickening from them, Psalm 119. 63. "I am a companion of all those who fear you" Good company quickens. The holy discourse and example of one saint—wets and sharpens another. The saints never go so fast to Heaven as when they go in company. One Christian helps another forward. In other races that are run, many times one hinders another; but in this race to Heaven, one Christian helps forward another. Thess. v. 11. "Edify one another, even as also you do" O let not this article of our creed be forgotten, "The communion of saints."

9. If you would be violent for Heaven—never leave until you have the Spirit. Desire of God to put forth the sweet violence of his Spirit; the spouse begged a gale of the Spirit, Cant. iv. 16. "Awake, O north wind, blow, O south." When God's Spirit blows upon us, then we go full sail to Heaven. When the Spirit of the living creatures was in the wheels, then they moved, Ezek. i. 21. The wheels of our endeavor move apace, when the Spirit of God is in these wheels. Seeing there are so many violent winds of temptation blowing us backward, we must have the violent wind of God's Spirit blowing us forward to Heaven. Let this suffice for speaking of the means for this holy violence.

Conclusion: What shall we do?

But some may say, we have used this violence for Heaven; what remains for us to do? As the people said to Christ, Luke i. 13. "What shall we do?"

You who have been violent for Heaven, and are now aged Christians, let me beseech you to still keep alive this holy violence. Not only keep up duty—but violence in duty. Remember, you have that corruption within you which is ready to abate this blessed violence. The brightest coal has those ashes growing on it, as are apt to choke the fire. You have those inbred corruptions, which, like ashes, are ready to choke the fire of your zeal. How was Peter's grace cooled when he denied Christ! The church of Ephesus lost her keen edge of piety, Rev. ii. 4. Take heed of declining in your affections. Be not like a body in an atrophy: be most violent to the last. You have but a little time now to work for God, therefore, work the harder. Be like the church of Thyatira; her "last works were more than her first," Rev. ii. 19. Be as the sun that shines brightest before its setting. Be as the swan that sings sweetest before its death. Rom xiii. 11. "Your salvation is nearer than when you believed." If your salvation be nearer, your violence should be greater. How should you quicken your pace, when you are within sight of the kingdom! He is a happy man of whom it may be said, spiritually, as of Moses literally before his death, Deut. xxxiv. 7. "His eyes waxed not dim and his natural force was not abated." So a Christian's force and violence for Heaven is not abated—he keeps the best wine of his life until last.

Here is strong consolation to the violent Christian—you are in the way to the kingdom. Though perhaps you have not much in the way, yet it is happy that you are in the way. Bless God that while some lie in the total neglect of duty, God has given you a heart to seek him, Psalm cv. 3. "Let the heart of them rejoice, who seek the Lord." Nay, God has not only given you a heart to do duty—but to do duty mixed with love—which makes it savory food; and to do duty stamped with fervency— which makes it pass current with God. O bless God who has raised you off the bed of sloth and stirred up the zeal of your soul for Heaven. He who has made you violent will make you victorious. Wait a while, and you shall possess the kingdom.

When Moses went up to receive God's commands, he stayed six days on the Mount, and on the seventh day God called him Exod. xxiv. 16. Though we wait long, and have not the thing waited for—yet let us continue doing our duty; shortly, God will call us from Heaven, "Come up here!" And we shall go from the mount of faith, to the mount of vision, and behold those glorious things which "eye has not seen, nor can it enter into man's heart to conceive."

But may a child of God may say, "I fear I am not one of those violent ones that shall take Heaven. I find such a deadness of heart in duty, that I question whether I shall ever arrive at the kingdom."

1. This deadness of heart may arise from natural causes. Weakness of body may occasion indisposition of mind. Your prayer may be weak, because your body is weak. A lute that is cracked cannot send forth so sweet a sound, as if it were whole.

2. This indisposition of soul perhaps is only casual, and for a time; it may be in a deep fit of melancholy, or in desertion. When the sun is gone from our climate, the earth is as it were in desertion, and the trees are without blossom or fruit; but this is only for a time. Let but the sun return again in Spring, and then the herbs flourish and the trees

put forth their fruit. So when God hides his face, there is a deadness upon a Christian's heart—he prays as if he prayed not. But let the Sun of Righteousness return, then he is divinely animated, and is as vigorous and lively in his operation as ever; he then recovers his first love. Therefore, weak Christian, be not discouraged, so long as you do not allow yourself in your distemper; a dead heart is your burden, look up to Christ your High-Priest, who is merciful to bear with your infirmities and is mighty to help them.

40539544R00044

Made in the USA
Middletown, DE
15 February 2017